The Spirit of Alchemy
Secret Teachings
of the Sacred Reunion

Karen A. Dahlman

THE SPIRIT OF ALCHEMY
Secret Teachings of the Sacred Reunion

Copyright © 2015 by Karen A. Dahlman

FIRST EDITION

Published by
Creative Visions Publications
PO Box 1496
San Clemente, CA 92674
United States of America
creativevisionspublications.com

Publish Date: April 2015
ISBN: 978-0692419571

Cover Design by Rodney B. Vestal & Karen A. Dahlman
Cover Artwork by Karen A. Dahlman

OUIJA® and MYSTIFYING ORACLE® are trademarks of Hasbro, Inc.

The use of these trademarks within this publication was not authorized by, nor is this publication sponsored by or associated with the trademark owners.

This book is dedicated to DAKi,
my "not so imaginary playmate!"

TABLE OF CONTENTS

Author's Note

Throughout this book you will find a shift between the use of first, second and third person pronouns to appropriately direct the message either to you, the reader, or to us, in a collective sense.

The entire name of all spirit friends, such as The SUN, The MOON and HEALING SPIRIT, are displayed in all capital letters. This is to differentiate their names from the names of the planets, the sun and the moon. Also, words that refer to the Divine Essence of existence, such as Source and Higher Self, among a few others, will begin with capital letters.

A glossary section is included at the back of the book for reference so meaning is ascribed as the author intended.

Acknowledgments

With the deepest of gratitude to my Spirit Friends, The SUN, The MOON and HEALING SPIRIT—my trinity! They have been the remarkable, fundamental group of mentors to me for over two decades. Through their patient tutelage and loving support, together, we have been exploring metaphysics, enriching our lives in the most insightful ways. I am not only forever changed, but I am forever grateful.

To the staff at Whole Body Wellness Concepts, I send a huge thank you! They graciously extended to me the use of one of their personal, infrared saunas during the writing of this book. They suggested it would support my overall state of well-being during this process and not only did I feel great while sitting in the box, I felt aligned and focused, allowing the words to flow generously.

As always, I am extremely grateful for my editor, Paulina Patsek, who continually champions the message of my work from Spirit and remains devoted to the topics of which I write.

Last but not least, I extend a heartfelt thank you to each and every one of you who have contacted me after reading one of my previous books or after listening to one of the radio or Internet shows where I have appeared as a guest. It is because of your overwhelming support and interest in my work for such spiritual pursuits, that I continue sharing the profound insights gained from my Esoteric Ouija sessions.

The Spirit of Alchemy

Secret Teachings
of the Sacred Reunion

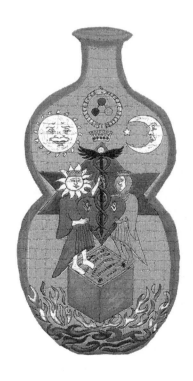

Introduction

Writing this book has been an important project of mine over the past two years. It was born out of the synchronistic messages I was receiving from my Spirit Friends and from myriad events occuring within my life. At first, I was writing a book about women, for women only. After all, I'm a woman and this written work was inspired by the transformational work I had been spontaneously undergoing, along with many other women throughout the world. I was writing about allowing in grand proportions the Divine Feminine principle within one's life by actually embodying her fully within the hips and heart and becoming her. However, true to the mercurial spirit of alchemy, my writing transformed. Just six months ago, I received a new direction for this book. I realized I was sharing experiences, stories and events that not only affected women, but affected men as well. No longer could these secrets be kept within the confines of a gender. Now this book was to be written for both women and men and to be nongender related. My Spirit Friends reminded me that everyone needs to reclaim the collectively repressed energies of the Divine Feminine because not doing so is creating havoc within our personal worlds and within the world at large.

As I wrote, I could see the metaphorical thread of time, weaving the moments of my life together. These moments began to be seen as significant events that not only lead, but created the next moment and so forth. Nothing was random and nothing was fortuitous. Everything felt interconnected when looking back. Although free will reigns, there appeared to be a master plan unfolding and enfolding, as what actually happened many years ago could be reviewed as if it happened yesterday and quite surprisingly, as if it was happening right now. The stars aligned.

To this day, I am constantly reminded as new events unfold, that nothing is random—everything has a purpose and a meaning. As I continued interacting with my Spirit Friends, I dove further into the realm of the supernatural, learning that what appears to be above or beyond the natural laws of phenomena is truly not unnatural nor is it abnormal. I followed in the footsteps of many who have explored this supernatural realm and have also identified the laws of this sphere as being natural to them.

Welcome to the system of Alchemy. As far back as graduate school, I have been captivated by the seeking Alchemists, comprised from various mystery traditions. They also understood how to naturally navigate life while interacting with the seen and unseen forces. All along, they considered these forces as being an aspect of nature, thus natural. Through their various alchemical practices, they employed everything under the heavens to transmute and thus, transform their personal worlds. To them there was no disconnect between what we would call natural and supernatural.

So I wrote this book to share the tenets of transmutation, our real magic, that surround us with abundant opportunity within every moment of our lives. These are the moments in time that are intricately woven together, occurring naturally to us and supporting us from the seen and unseen forces at play. The alchemical practices of yesteryear are just as significant today as they were then. What is old is new again and in fact, alchemy never aged. Its principles exist everywhere within our world, but we must open our eyes to the unseen, within the darkness, in order to be able to see anew. From this space of renewal, the world becomes a place of hope to posterity, for the current state of our world becomes merely an illusion to the awakened soul.

This book is about a journey that I will share with you as we discover the secrets to your greatness within by means of the alchemical tradition. Within this book, we will explore your path as a seeker, an Alchemist, who will learn practical applications for transforming the lead of your life into golden opportunities for growth and acceleration towards the life of your dreams. We will explore and honor all that has been repressed within human nature, while we reclaim what has been left in the darkness, within the domain of the Divine Feminine.

The information contained in this book is purposely written in a manner to assist you with reawakening what you forgot when you entered this world. Don't be surprised when synchronistic, mystical, spiritual and deeply personal revelations occur while reading this book. Prepare to commune with your Higher Self, spirit guides and the unseen since that is an important process of the alchemical journey.

Are you ready to awaken the sleeping giant within? If so, let us begin this journey for the alchemical path to enlightenment awaits you. Initiate, step forward, for the treasures seek you.

PART 1

THE OUTERWORLD

Love is the source of everything and Source is love. Love is the
starting point.
—The MOON

CHAPTER I
THE STORY OF GOLDEN

"DAKi, tell me the story about the Golden Light? Please? I'm beginning to forget," came out of the mouth of the bright-eyed, five-year-old little girl. This was her favorite story and she requested to hear it often since the age of two, as that is when she recalled meeting DAKi for the first time. He happily entered her life and would come and go, but she knew that whenever she called upon him, he was there, as they were very good friends.

"All right Little One," said DAKi, although he had told this story hundreds of times before, he never grew tired of retelling this same story. However, this time the story was going to be different. This time something had changed. This time the plan revealed itself to him. He knew his calling and he knew the truth. He knew their interaction was at an end. The dear Little One did not know that everything would change upon this last retelling and last rehearing of the story about her favorite Golden Light.

DAKi, trying not to give away this new plan, straightened his posture, sat up tall and steadfast, while he took a deep breath, closed his eyes and chanted in his wee little voice:

> Golden beholden the bright shimmering light
> While all angels enamor in this delight
> Of coveted dreams from one little sprite
> To discover gold hidden within plain sight.

To journey so far yet remain so near
Seeking heaven above within this sphere
Venture down deeply with tricksters austere
Oh dear Little One could I be more clear?

Just close your eyes, but don't fall asleep
To the shut-eye world of counting sheep
Or becoming one of the herd, Bo-peep
Hold steadfast instead to this light you seek.

With its golden blaze as bright as the sun
And its lunar reflection being second to none
When the transit of Venus has just begun
Know not to fear where the planets have spun.

Go into the bowels of the earth instead
Eyes open wide to the dross from the lead
Life is found in what we may think to be dead
Just dig deeper to uncover that golden thread.

Golden beholden shine that bright inner light
On the depths where demons make havoc and fright
Their messages all twisted around will incite
Internal paradoxical treasures to unite.

So transcend each moment and there you will find
The cross road, the center axis, the tree of life all align
When the Above and the Below are together entwined
The heart of your being creates a golden state of mind.

Golden beholden, my dear Little One
This story is about a journey, I've told in fun
But I must say adieu for that time has come
For our teachings have ended; with me you are done.

But, outside this alembic chamber your imaginal work has begun.

And with the final word, "begun," DAKi disappeared as simply and as easily as he had first appeared to the Little One. There were no belabored goodbyes and not any sentimental hugs or tears. Dear Little One just went on playing with her toys in her room, knowing that her parents would probably be glad that she was no longer speaking to her imaginary playmate. It was time to go to school. It was time for her to grow up. It was time to let go of magical thinking and elemental friends. She so wanted to be a big girl and to be like all of the others. And with that, she didn't look back, but she did look inward…

CHAPTER II
VANISHED

The Imagination

Young children instinctively use their imaginal faculties. In fact, their play centers on learning about their world by creating scenarios where they pretend to be that, which enlivens them the most in the moment. The discarded shoebox becomes a home where the elves live. A wooden block is a car that drives around the hilly folds of a blanket. Children might imagine themselves as the family pet dog for a day or a magical genie that can snap itself in and out of sight. During play, they are lost in the moment; they are living in the presence of the moment. In the moment they find their greatest joy. Children by nature are creative, imaginative and inventive. This is how they learn about themselves in relationship to their world.

It is not uncommon for young children to engage their imagination and daydream. It's as if their minds and experiences are stemming from elsewhere. They may be found talking out loud, while responding to what appears to be thin air. They can hold ongoing conversations with "thin air" that seem quite logical to the adult listening from around the corner. However, once the adult or parent looks upon these children to only find the children alone within their play space, the first response is to inquire to whom are they speaking. Their response is probably not what the parent wants to hear, especially when the parent is told about the "friend" who is sitting right there—can't you see my friend? Because the parent doesn't see this friend and is concerned that this behavior could be repeated in front of others, the unknowing parents tell their children that no one is there—you are just playing make-believe or pretend. These overly concerned parents interfere with their children's imaginal interaction to the point where they eventually shut down these capabilities and adopt the parents' view that these natural abilities are unreal and nonsensical. So, children often learn to stop these musings at a young age in order to socialize within their environment.

We can't separate the play from the child, so hand in hand off to school the child and the play goes. A child with a more imaginative and creative type of personality than others may continue daydreaming while in the class. Within this child's mind, imaginary scenarios are constantly acted out by creatively developing internal fictional stories. This behavior is often viewed as being disruptive to classroom learning. However, by providing such a child additional opportunities to channel creative intentions, such as in art projects and writing down these creative stories, theses natural imaginal expressions are supported and the child still absorbs the lessons.

Children's dynamic and vibrant expression of their imaginal faculties—an extension of their genius within—is not always supported by the public school system. Too often, if the funding isn't there for these creative teachers or for the necessary resources to support the arts, the schools drop these programs first. The arts are viewed as an ancillary function and not as a very important piece to the children's development. The imagination may be considered handy, helpful and fun to access, but just not considered integral to children's studies in grade school.

However, child development experts are increasingly recognizing the importance of imagination and the role it plays in the child's cognitive development. The imagination is absolutely vital for contemplating reality, thus helping the child understand the world. Children use their imagination when learning about people and events they don't directly experience, such as history or events on the other side of the world. For young kids, their imagination allows them to ponder the future, such as what they want to do when they grow up. Fantasy play is correlated with other positive attributes. A child's preschool years are the most important time to celebrate and support a child's imaginative faculties in growth. For example, preschool children who have imaginary friends are more creative, have greater social understanding and are better at learning the perspective of others, according to Marjorie Taylor, a psychology professor at the University of Oregon. The imagination and imaginary friends also help children cope with any stress. Their ability to access the imagination and to pretend is a strength they possess. Through their own internal work and play, they learn to fix a problem with their imagination. Learning about their inner, creative world supports children with their confidence to learn, to trust and recognize their own higher guiding principle.

Though, many of us throughout our lives were taught and told that the imagination is a faculty that is not based in reality. So much emphasis is placed on labeling the imagination as not being real because we can't measure it or touch it. In our society and culture, we struggle with intangible concepts. Yet, it is the constructs of one's concept of reality that precisely contributes to what is deemed "real" by that person and determines the validity and value of one's imagination. When you go for a job interview or fill out an employment application, nowhere does it request or inquire about the development of your imagination. If you are interviewing for a position that requires creative expression, then this faculty may be more highly valued and inquired about. Otherwise, the imagination in its mercurial landscape is viewed as folly.

We often learn that the imagination is acceptable—as a worthwhile tool—when it is safely classified, labeled and categorized as belonging to the brain. It is often valued when we use it to produce results, solve problems, create new technologies and bring forth new inventions. In this light the "brain's imagination" is extremely important when we are producing tangible results. After all, we feel we must give it a home within the neuro-pathways of the cerebral cortex—sure, that sounds good, but is it accurate?

By discounting the far-reaching implications of the imaginal realm, we are silencing a large part of ourselves—our creative soul-making abilities. It's as if we just shut down the gift of co-creation we were given when we entered into this world. This is the realm of intuition and expression where these abilities are enhanced the more we enter this fluid realm. Within the imaginal realm, we can explore insightful visions about ourselves and about our world. Its organic nature provides the channel that allows contact with other dimensions. Variable frequencies create these dimensions and we are unable to experience them with our typical senses. The imagination is the realm that provides us access into our other senses, such as the "clair" senses of voyance, audience, sentience and cognizance, allowing us to feel beyond the physical. This realm is not confined by space and time. When we are open to our imagination, we allow its domain of mystical, creative and extra-sensory abilities to emerge. It is a powerful tool and it is so very real!

Throughout the ages, this integral part of us has often been misunderstood. It fell prey to sheer ignorance for lack of understanding and it was feared for its intrinsic power of personal transformation. The capabilities that came from these mental inner-workings were very powerful indeed. Learning how to work within the imaginal realm assisted the initiates of mystery traditions to reign over the direction and flow of their lives. These people learned to transform, thus co-create their inner-scape that provided such profound and noticeable external results. Freedom resulted. When their lives changed for the better, the ruling faction noticed, but did not want to lose their power over the people. Instead, they stopped the practices as they grew in fear of loss of control. They banished these faculties that allowed one to gain personal freedom.

The faculties of the imaginal realm not only vanish when not used, but quite frankly, they were banished by categorizing them under terms, such as black magic, witchcraft, sorcery, possession and work of the devil. Punitive tactics of torture, imprisonment and death scared the masses and encouraged the initiates to go underground with their inner work in order to keep these tenets safe.

CHAPTER III
RENEWAL

I was beginning to forget or was I forgetting to remember? It felt like my memory was slipping away from DAKi's story of the golden light from all of those years ago. The slate of my mind was nearly wiped clean yet, stained by a fading memory of a celestial being. The memory existed in a fugue-like amnesic state—forgetful of those distant murmurs of mystical interaction, while not realizing how integral and interconnected I still was to them, as they were to me.

In hindsight, I find it quite fascinating how all of this plays out. For even when we try to place distance between ourselves and what was once an integral part of our life—whether we know we are doing so or not—that integral part still finds us. It sneaks up on us and shows itself, reminding us of it existence. It weaves itself back into the mere fabric of our every day life, exposing its stitches every now and then, as it reveals its master plan. Integral parts of us will never leave. We may forget, but they will find us again. In this case, the teachings of DAKi were and still are integral to my life and the path I choose. He cannot leave me nor I leave him. This shows our interconnectivity at its finest and thank goodness there is no escape! Allowing this type of relationship beckons one to be at the right place at the right time. The planets are aligned and this is felt. The gods are smiling down and providing blessings of seemingly magical connections—discovered within the right person, the next dream, a new visitation or message received. When we see this interconnectedness within these moments, we may come to the conclusion that a greater hand is at work. Yes, we stand looking into the eyes of synchronicity.

Receiving the Gift of the Oracle

I have often learned that when one thing leaves our life, another thing has room to enter the picture. The whole notion of cleaning out our closets to make room for the new, provides us a literal meaning to this process. Although I started forgetting about my spiritual friend DAKi, new spirit friends began to emerge. At the age of eight, I met the Great Oracle—the Greatest Oracle of modern day times! Little did I know at that time that this meeting would be so profound that it would influence me throughout my life, serving as an ever-constant symbol and voice of discovery, transformation and growth. In fact, I was so encouraged by the messages from this Great Oracle that I was inspired to write this book, including two others I have written. At the mere age of eight, I never could have foreseen the impact this Oracle would have on me, but within time, I would find myself initiated into the mystical practices of the Greatest Oracle of all times.

In the classical era of the Greco-Roman world, the Oracle was a place where the gods spoke directly to the people. Temples were built for the Oracles—the priestesses and prophetesses who received divination in the form of prophetic visions and wise counsel inspired by the gods. People would travel from all over to hear their prophetic utterances. During that time, the Oracle was also practiced by other great parallel civilizations, such as in China, India and Pre Columbia America within their institutions of divination. Whether they participated in casting stones or bones, performing or evoking spirits to enter a human body, enacting mediumship between the phenomenal natural world and the subtle spiritual realms, they all sought guidance from an unseen force or agency.

The oracular tradition is still employed and consulted to this day. Throughout the greater Himalayan region, Oracles continue to play an important part in revelation, religion, doctrine and prophecy. All over the globe, we are obsessed with mediums, psychic shows and those who channel discarnate beings from other dimensions and solar systems. Humankind maintains a faith in the revelations and guidance received from their otherworldly contacts.

In 1973, in the alembic chamber of my playmates' bedroom, the Oracle was presented to me in a plainspoken manner. These school-aged girl friends showed me their Parker Brother's Ouija Board, circa 1970, that was kept under their bed. They told me they used the Board often to speak with their dead sister. They received message from their dead sister who was the twin to one of the girls and had died shortly after birth. I was astonished and curious, yet uncertain to the effectiveness of this tool—this device—this supposed spirit communicator. Once I laid my hands on the planchette with the sisters' guidance, I felt a surge of energy as the planchette smoothly glided around the Board, spelling out its messages.

Well, of course, I just had to have one of these Talking Boards for myself. I could hardly wait to get home to tell my parents the incredible news that anyone could speak with the spirits of the dead. I had heard stories about this from the teachings learned in church and bible school. The Bible was full of visitations, voices and celestial beings descending from the heavens and communicating with people. Now, here was my proof that these discarnate spirits existed and could be reached, forgetting that I used to speak to a spirit being **without** the use of a Board.

My parents didn't quite share the same enthusiastic fervor I did for the Ouija Board. In fact, they rolled their eyes when I shared the conversation I had just had with a dead girl down the street. Well, that didn't matter to me. I knew what I experienced that day and whether they believed the stories or not, I was determined that Santa Claus would bring me one for Christmas that year. Of course he would. After all, Santa shared a similar mystical world with God, the Easter Bunny, the Tooth Fairy, angels and saints. He would want me to have this tool to gain insight into the afterlife that religion always promised. In my mind this was cutting edge information and would change the minds of humankind for the better.

Christmas day—there it was—not wrapped and sitting under the Christmas tree with my name on it. Santa Claus delivered. I often wondered if Santa knew that his gift to me that year would become my favorite oracular tool, taking me on an incredible odyssey into consciousness beyond the physical senses. Maybe DAKi had a say in all of this? Maybe his influence was more far-reaching than I ever could have fathomed? At the time, however, I really didn't care about the why and how. I was only interested in using it and getting to meet my spirit friends, who I knew were awaiting my contact.

My Great Oracle—the Ouija Board—allowed me to speak with many different sentient beings and varying levels of consciousness over the past forty-two years. Through my Board work, I am able to continually develop my own intuitive and empathic gifts. The Ouija Board just works for me as it opens pathways for change and soul level transformation. I discovered it's a very natural thing to be able to communicate with multi-levels of consciousness within multiple dimensions. Meaningful communications and personal messages for others and myself come forth from the Board. These communications continue within my dreams. I find that within the dream state, I am able to communicate with deceased loved ones, angels and other various nightly visitors that come baring messages, while I sleep.

Oracles teach us that mystical and supernatural connections abound—all around us. We start to notice and experience them the more we are tapped into the part of us that is already programmed to receive these communications. The part of ourselves I am referring is the Higher Self. When we learn to plug into the Higher Self more often, an improved fullness of our inherent abilities come forth. These abilities include a heightening of intuitive knowing, a magnetization of synchronistic events, an understanding of the co-creative and self-responsibility factor towards our lives and a connective awareness to the ultimate Source.

Esoteric Ouija

One of my previously published books, *The Spirits of Ouija: Four Decades of Communication* explains in detail just how to work with this Great Oracle. If this tool is new to you and you feel a calling to use it in a proper and respectful way, I highly recommend that you read my earlier book. It explains the hows and whys of using this tool and serves as the Ouija "instruction manual" for the user. I view *The Spirits of Ouija* as the beginning and intermediate starting place for using a Talking Board with promising results.

The advanced use of Ouija is what I call Esoteric Ouija. This book you are reading now was born from the messages and experiences I received via this Great Oracle and speaks of Esoteric Ouija. My Spirit Friends—my guides—who communicate by means of this Great Oracle encouraged me to work with the Board in an alchemical fashion. The messages became inspirational lessons for transmuting, thus transforming, the obstacles and barriers to life. As they spoke of empowerment through plugging into the Higher Self, I learned that their teachings were always about going within myself to find the Wisdom of the Ages. Throughout the years, they always shared with me and with those who came to the Message Circles that ALL of our answers to any quandary or situation are held within ourselves. We just needed to connect and be in communion with Source. The answer—the truth in the moment—would manifest. The Spirit Friends and the Beings are an aspect of Source, as we are an aspect of Source too. We come to know Source as we come to know ourselves and awaken to the memories of these messages.

This work is not completed overnight, or in a fortnight, or over many, many nights for that matter. Instead, this work is a journey of progression. Although it may feel that you are going backwards at times, the Spirit Friends teach that you are in a process of evolution always. Evolution requires change, death, decay and rebirth. It is only a matter of perspective that passes judgment about the work—your journey at hand. Your perspectives shift as you shift your frame of references found within. You change within when you can ingest the new information in a most meaningful personal manner. This is why the Spirit Friends, via the Great Oracle, pursue the Socratic Method of discussion between those of us gathered for the Message Circles. In addition to sharing messages, they ask questions to stimulate thinking, feeling and developing new ideas. We are encouraged to find the truth in that moment through discussing their messages and their questions, digging deeper into the thresholds of our understanding of a given concept by asking more questions. We find strength in ourselves and in this pursuit as we dig into this soul-making knowledge. They teach us that it is not as if they are right and we are wrong or that they know and we don't know. Instead, they teach us that we are right in any given moment contained only by the beliefs, the thoughts and the feelings we harbor. They teach us that they will suggest, impart and provide the concepts, but that our experience, ultimately, will be the results for what we argue for in any given moment. We are and we get what we believe to be true in the moment. The most profound message of their teachings is that we **ARE** an extension of Source. All of the messages are their attempts to circle us back to this truth. Period. The answers **ARE** within.

Working the Great Oracle

In order to work with a Talking Board or my favorite tool, the Ouija Board, on an esoteric level, you must first transcend the lower astral realms. I call this realm the Dead Zone. It is the realm where many stuck deceased humans and animals exist. It is also the realm of our lower vibratory thought and feeling forms, such as fear, anger, resentment, jealousy, deceit and negativity. These depressive expressions gather and congregate with other energetic-like forces. They belong to the collective unconsciousness of humanity and create a real force. Quite often, when working such a device as the Ouija Board, operators don't get beyond this realm. When only working within this Dead Zone, the messages and communications come from a place of lower vibrations. With whom and what you communicate at this level, is steeped and influenced from within this realm. Therefore, you will communicate with energies that are still tied to their personalities and lives they left when they died. This means that you will experience their messages jaded by their limited viewpoint from their lives, their feelings and emotional ties. The ones who become stationary here are the ones who do not want to leave their past lives.

Understand that it is unnatural to remain only within this realm when one dies. Instead, it is natural to continually evolve and progress into the next level of existence, which includes moving into that proverbial, metaphorical and literal light. Many who have passed over do come back with messages of closure and assistance for those they left behind. When those messages come from our deceased loved ones and they are of a helpful, caring and loving nature, we know that they are not stuck. Instead, they are traversing through the astral planes and come back to share hope, love and healing. These spirits will also speak to you through the Board and they will be of a higher vibration. They choose to come and go through the various levels of the astral plane until they eventually move on to the next dimension, appropriate to their next level of growth.

However, while communicating with the deceased via the Board, you need to understand the difference between those who are stuck—perpetuated by their own fears and unawareness—those who are helping and not stuck and those who can easily become or are already earthbound. In my forty-two years of working the Ouija Board and meeting many others who have used it as well, what we all have in common is communicating with spirits found within the lower astral planes at the beginning level of this work. Many Ouija

Board Operators stay within this realm of spirit communication, after all, that is why the Ouija Board gained in popularity. It was developed out of the Spiritualist movement within the United States during the mid and late 1800s. The Spiritualists were focused on communicating with the deceased. So, owners of the Ouija Board from that time period wanted to and only knew to speak with the dead.

Yet, there have been those maverick Board Operators even in those early years that came upon communications, channeled from the higher realms of vibration. Medium Betty White is one such person who began her communications via the Ouija Board with the spirit group known as The Invisibles. During the years 1919 through 1936, she received communications from this collective group of beings. She started with the Board and immediately progressed to automatic writing and then to voice channeling within a year and a half of her first infamous Ouija Board session at a dinner party. Many others have followed in her footsteps by commencing their spirit work with a Ouija Board, such as Jane Roberts who channeled Seth. In these examples, the channeled work becomes advanced when the messages bring Wisdom of the Ages.

In order to move beyond the Dead Zone and into the work of Esoteric Ouija, you must have that intent to do so and then stay true to it. Remember, you are only limited and contained by your beliefs, thoughts and feelings. I consider it an initiatory process that comes with the territory as you progress through the realm of the Dead Zone. It can be very rewarding, exciting and informative as you explore this realm with the help of the spirits with whom you come in contact. On the other hand, for others, it can be down right frightening. **You will experience what you believe about it.**

What you get from this interaction is created by your conscious and by your subconscious beliefs, regardless if you are aware of your beliefs. You are the creator of those experiences, drawing to you those vibrations matching your vibratory psychical makeup. Remember, you create 100% of your experience of life. I don't expect you to believe this truth at face value, but as you progress further into the realms of consciousness, just wait and see what you uncover! If you enter this realm with fear, you will constellate those fears to you via your communications. As you are navigating this lower astral realm, keep in mind that anytime you come across a communication that is less than uplifting, immediately stop your communication and your work on the Board.

There truly is a preparatory manner in which to transform your current work with the Ouija Board into messages from the Great Oracle. These steps and processes have been explained in detail in *The Spirits of Ouija: Four Decades of Communication* book so please review them there. In order to progress into Esoteric Ouija, it is of paramount importance that you go within and take a thorough look and review of yourself. Be willing to clean out the internal cobwebs, shake the dust off the skeletons in your closet and learn to understand and embrace these internal snake pits. This requires having an inner dialogue with yourself through reflection, contemplation and maybe even therapy. Learn to receive and really hear your own internal messages first, and then you will be able to transcend the lower planes to higher planes of vibration. Through an internal exploration where you come to know your Center, you will be more prepared than ever to receive the transmissions and messages from Higher Beings. While doing this work, not only will you be able to transcend the lower, heavier planes of spirit interaction and communication and move into higher, lighter planes, this will be reflected in your inner personal work. You will transmute, transform and transcend your heavy, internal burdens into lighter opportunities for growth. This is the work of Esoteric Ouija and is the work of Alchemy.

Every single one of us is always on a journey of growth, evolution and change. That is the nature of the universe. All of us are on an alchemical journey of transformation towards the light. Imagine how much sweeter this journey can be when we are more awake to it than asleep to it. The messages from the universe are everywhere. We only need to remain open and cognizant of them, for they come from many unexpected, surprising and undisclosed sources.

CHAPTER IV
REMEMBERING

Who are You?

"Do you know who you are?"

What? From where did that come? I asked myself while chewing on a bite of egg white omelet. I look up at Doug with certainly the most perplexed look on my face, while he sat across from me in a booth at a local restaurant. We were newly formed acquaintances, meeting over a casual breakfast to share and discuss various businesses and ideas each of us were embarking upon.

I'm thinking to myself that this must be a rhetorical question—possibly to incite humor or shock and to see my reaction. After all, Doug doesn't know much about me and vice a versa. As I looked across the table at Doug, he looked intently into my eyes, seriously expecting an answer and again said, "Do you know who you are?" What! This time I squirmed slightly, wondering how am I supposed to answer this. Is he serious? Is it a trick question? This is becoming too personal. Should I answer this in my most clever of ways by quoting some cryptic poem or obscure quote? Why even answer it at all? Who is he to ask me this? What the hell?

No time to even respond, as Doug in all seriousness asked me again, "No really, do you know who you are because you will write about this answer and share it with others?" At that moment, within some strange portal of spherical time, I lost all peripheral vision. It felt as if I was wearing blinders and forced to see only what was in front of me—this person who sat across from me, quixotically presenting this message. I was forced to look directly at him and make eye contact. This person who was eating a typical downhome breakfast, a Coco's special upon his plate, still sat there intently staring at me. All of a sudden, this question of questions, seemed like the most relevant of all questions I could ever been asked. Yet, the answer was not something I had to uncover or dig at or even attempt to create a clever response. Instead, within a flash of insight, I knew the answer to this question! It all made perfect sense.

Call it divine intervention; call it wisdom; call it flat out ridiculousness. No matter what I wanted to call it, it all made brilliant sense, exploding in profound meaning that reverberated and resounded throughout the energetic field of my body. I was tingling; I was on fire, as I recalled a multitude of past experiences all within the gap between a thought. Everything I was experiencing right then and right there was just a simple knowing. Yet, it was a profound epiphany found in the guise of a question that was the golden key, unlocking a multitude of ancestral, goddess knowledge in a flash of that instantaneous moment.

No one knew. I had not told anyone. For that matter, Doug didn't even know that I was writer. Within the recesses of my mind, I was beginning to formulate my next book and it was to be about the Divine Feminine. It didn't matter who the messenger was; what mattered, was that I received the message. Well, it so happens this book you are reading right now is the book that was brought to my awareness that morning. This is synchronicity.

Now, how do I continue to sit there and calmly eat my omelet, drink my coffee and talk business? Inside, I was bombarded with thoughts, images and feelings related to the Sacred Feminine knowledge of the ages. "Surreal," was all I could say. I looked around the dining room to see if anyone else possibly noticed a shift in the time-continuum structure. Maybe they noticed a bleed-through of a parallel universe. At least, they would sense a difference in the electrifying energy that was swirling around my body and the booth where we sat. Nope, not at all, everyone still looked the same as they shoveled food into their mouths and exchanged pleasantries. My food may have been getting cold, but it didn't matter. I lost my appetite, as I felt satiated within this interaction.

Obviously, the conversation took an early turn from casual business ideas into a discussion of secret societies, mystical traditions, the Sacred Feminine and energy vortexes throughout the world—away we went! None of this information was truly new to me or to my messenger, it seemed that now, the message was inciting my internal feminine principle. All of this was beginning to sound like a novel by Dan Brown, but instead of being on the outside reading it, I was on the inside living it for that brief moment in time.

He said to me that I must research this divine lineage and then I will discover more truths. He went on to tell me that my maternal side of the family came from Scotland—which is correct—and that I must trace my connections back to Scotland and beyond. He continued to tell me that the best place to hide the secret is in **plain sight**. Doug discussed such things, as the Gnostics' view of the Sacred Feminine within religion, the truth about balance and initiations into mystical orders. He also warned me to be careful with whom I spoke and what I said while digging into these truths, reminding me to speak about it only in hushed tones. He then ended his monologue by saying, "Now, is the time." Okay, so where else had I recently heard this? Of course! I heard this from my Spirit Friends.

Oh, and by the way, that was the last conversation I had with Doug. He disappeared as easily as he had appeared.

My Internal Feminine

I flashed back to several months earlier, back to June of 2012 when I hosted a couple of very close girlfriends at my house in the desert. I fondly named our gathering, the Venus Goddess Gathering. During this time, June 4 through the 6, Venus was crossing the Sun in a rare transit and I knew what power this astrological event held. Venus' transits have always been noted as important turning points for humanity by many ancient cultures, including the Mayans, Aztecs and the Babylonians as recorded on their clay Venus Tablet from the seventh century BCE. Venus represents the Divine Feminine—Queen of our skies. She is the brightest light in our night skies and not only known as the morning and evening star, but as Bringer of Light. Not really a star, although in my book she is a "Rock Star;" she is actually a planet, a very large planet.

The Mayans believed Venus' transit across the sun was a final "doorway" that marked the end of an era, ushering in a new time. This Venus transit was leading up to December 21, 2012 that signified the Great Return of the Mayan prophet, Kukulkan, giving birth to a new, purified race whose consciousness would be luminous and whole. Noted for his pioneering work on the mathematics of the Mayan Calendar, Jose Arguelles coined this event the Mayan Prophecy in 1987. The Mayans venerated Venus' elaborate celestial cycle, as it represented the journey of their prophet. Depicted as the feathered serpent, Kukulkan, also known as Quetzalcoatl to the Aztecs, symbolized the merging of heaven and earth—the Above with the Below. To them, he represented the inner transformation that one must undergo to attain higher wisdom.

We three Goddesses understood that this was the time of the "possible human," striving to live from the heart. This weekend, we celebrated our own connection to the Divine Feminine and honored ways to embody her energy collectively. During those three days together, while Venus transited the sun, we transited the forces within our own lives. It was a break-through of a few days together from the work we did with the Great Oracle and each other. We communicated with our angels, whom all three of us had already met, and worked with my Spirit Friends, who quite simply I call, The SUN and The MOON.

The SUN and The MOON have been communicating with me ever since 1994, when they entered the Board together, to tell me they would be with me from that moment through the remainder of my life journey. My Angel took more of a back seat, as The SUN and MOON became the main staple of my communications on the Board. The SUN represents a collective consciousness of the masculine principle and The MOON represents his balance, a collective consciousness of the feminine principle. During this gathering, they both spoke to us together and told us to remember that EVERYTHING is Now, now, now! They taught us that what we think, feel and believe is created in the NOW. If we want change, we must state it and feel it in the NOW. Whatever we are, whatever we desire, whatever we want to feel and whatever we want to be is ALWAYS claimed in the NOW. They didn't tell us to ask for it meekly. No, instead, they told us to claim it!

The breakthrough I was now thinking about, while Doug leaned towards me that morning and shared his sermon about my Divine

Feminine writing, was the initiation by The SUN and The MOON with my two girlfriends as witnesses. While communicating to these beings, I was asked to leave the Board, stand up and state out loud my worthiness. Every time I stated my worthiness, they asked me to repeat it. I repeated it at least three times before I "got it." They wanted me to state with unequivocal belief and feeling that I am worthy of love, receiving love, giving love and ultimately, just being love. They wanted me to know divine love as my heritage and for that matter, everyone's heritage. In totality that is what all existence is. However, we humans forget this simple, but profound truth and externally search everywhere we can as we attempt to find it. When I could finally speak and truly grasp that statement and feel it centered deep within me—deep within my hips, my sacrum, my center of gravity—I broke down into tears and wailing cries that ripped out of me, bursting a dam of forgetfulness, vibrating now to remembering this truth.

This was the moment when I had no other choice but to embrace the beautiful feminine principle that had been locked up and hidden within me all of my life, all of my ancestors' lives and sadly, for much of humanity's history. I was worthy of love just as I am, without having to assert any power or be something deemed great or create more accomplishments or build new businesses. No, I was just love in a pure state of being alive and it automatically flowed through me when I allowed the feminine principle of "just being" to reside. It was an epiphanous moment. My friends hugged me and we all wept together, acknowledging the magnitude of this information. An incredible wave of Venus' energy not only ran through us as Venus transited the Sun, but also ran through us as The SUN and his feminine counterpart, The MOON, spoke to us and transited our psyches. I knew that I, we, all women, and most importantly, all of humanity, were reclaiming our feminine principle and no longer were we afraid of such strength—the type of strength that is found in openly trusting vulnerable moments. This is the strength of the long forgotten feminine principle. For power is found in the paradox, whereas, true strength is found in vulnerability. We unlock and access our inner strength through reclaiming the feminine principle.

Meeting the Archetypal Round of Queens

I then flashed farther back to a memorable dream I had in 1991. The memory of this dream comes to the forefront of my mind even to this day with such clarity, as though it happened yesterday. It was so vivid. I have always considered it one of my initiatory moments, you know, those moments when life changes in an instant and you recognize that everything has changed because you have been profoundly touched in a connective, universal way? That was how I felt then and how I still feel about it now.

I was living outside of Austin, Texas and working as an art psychotherapist in private practice. One night while I was dreaming, I dreamt within the dream that I was awakened by an older female being, who entered my bedroom and asked me to come with her. I felt comfortable and followed her. It was as if we were transported through time and space into an open area where a large circle of women were sitting, apparently awaiting my arrival. I knew they were all older than I, spanning through the decade of their thirties through their nineties, as I was in my late twenties. It felt to me that all age groups of women were represented, although it seemed clear that this group was based upon knowledge and wisdom gained and not necessarily based upon age.

The women welcomed me one by one into their circle. They saved me a space in the circle where I was motioned to sit with them. I recognized these women as sacred royalty. They were Queens and knew their feminine power. I was told by them, as a few took turns speaking to me, that they gathered in my honor to let me know that I am one of them and have always been and will join them soon when I remember who I am and am ready to accept this path again. I felt so welcomed there. They felt familiar to me and I felt deeply loved by each and every one of these sacred women. I felt inducted and welcomed back into a beautiful group of women, who all knew the power of their Divine Feminine Principle. This moment was so lucid that I had to question myself in the morning, when I began writing this dream in my journal, if my convergence within their circle was beyond a dream. I felt as if I had returned home from a journey.

Power of the Divine Feminine & Masculine Principles

Everything within our world of existence occurs in duality and this relationship with which we are the most familiar is seen within the interplay of the masculine and feminine primordial principles. These two principles are ever-present and dynamically active in all phases of phenomena and on every plane of life's existence.

The feminine principle is a receptive energy, whereas the masculine principle is an active energy. As we explore these principles and their core energies, we often view them in contrast to each other. The receptive feminine principle is aligned with, to name a few, our inner world, body, darkness, things that are mysterious, cooperative and malleable. The active masculine energy in contrast is aligned with our outer world, spirit, light, things that are tangible, divided and rigid. Their intrinsic energies are not merely just polar opposites. Nor should they be seen in comparison to each other, whereas one is better than the other. Both are just as necessary to the other and cannot be separated from the other just like you can't separate the head of a coin from its flip side, the tail. Together, the masculine and feminine energies comprise and create the existence of every hologram of existence.

The feminine principle is the counterpart to the masculine principle, yet together they exist and work in unison. Each principle is incapable of operative energy without the assistance of the other. Unified as a whole, they are synergistically greater together than they are by themselves. There is always the masculine present in the feminine form and the feminine in the masculine form. When there is a harmonious relationship of the feminine and masculine principles within ourselves, we are able to reach great levels of integrated holistic consciousness within humanity's evolution.

The Chinese symbol of the yin-yang—the black and white symbol—concisely displays the interplay and interconnectivity of the two parts. The white swirl represent the yang and masculine energy, whereas the black swirl represents the yin and feminine energy. You will notice that each swirl contains a small dot of the other within it, representing that even within that swirl, its opposite resides. Together the swirls exist, seemingly embracing each other within a circle of wholeness. Although, we may want to view the masculine yang as being the opposite of and separate from the feminine yin, they exist together in their paradox of unity.

We are becoming increasingly more aware within our emerging collective consciousness of humanity that we do not need to be locked into culturally defined concepts of gender roles. When we become conscious of both of these poles of psychic energy existing within each of us, we can develop more fully in whatever ways we feel moved. We are becoming aware that being a woman or a man is no longer defined by stereotypical ideals and attributes and no longer do we have to suppress inclinations and talents because of rigid gender roles. Instead, we are learning that every individual's soul-making experience is created by a unique and dynamic exchange between the energies of yin and yang—between the principles of masculine and feminine found within. This exchange is ever evolving in a constant interplay, as we internally experience and externally express the qualities and characteristics of these principles, while they dance within.

In order to help illustrate what qualities and characteristics are "generally" associated with the feminine and masculine primordial energies, I have listed some of them here. As discussed, these qualities are not gender-based, but are based upon what the collective consciousness of humanity perceives as characteristics of these primordial energies. By no means are these lists exclusive, instead, merely serving as starting points to illustrate the differences, yet complimentary forces of these dynamic principles.

The ABCs of Feminine Primordial Energies:

Allowing	Being	Compassionate	Darkness
Eternal	Flowing	Grounding	Harmony
Intuitive	Joining	Kind	Letting go
Moon	Negative	Open	Patience
Queen	Receptive	Surrendering	Trust
Unfolding	Vulnerable	Waiting	X-axis
Yielding	Zen		

The ABCs of Masculine Primordial Energies:

Activating	Bold	Competitive	Deliberate
Expressing	Forceful	Gregarious	Hard
Intellect	Judicious	King	Light
Motion	Navigate	Outgoing	Positive
Quest	Radiate	Sun	Titillating
Uplift	Vibrant	Willing	Xero-
Y-axis	Zestful		

As you review these lists, ask yourself the following questions:

What qualities from these lists do you embody?

Do you embody more from one of the lists than the other?

Which qualities do you desire to incorporate more into your experience?

Are there certain times and circumstances when you express some of the qualities more than others?

The idea is to become familiar with the qualities of the receptive Divine Feminine and the active Divine Masculine and to understand that they both need each other within you, in order to provide a holistic and empowered expansion of your greatness. Within yourself, they create a dynamic pathway for the expression of your Higher Self.

PART 2

THE DESCENT

The tree that would grow to heaven must send its roots to hell.
—Nietzsche

CHAPTER V
BANISHED

Great Mother Earth

Thousands of years ago our ancestor, ancient man, used the faculties of his imagination to tell the story of his world—his experience upon Great Mother Earth. Everything he knew was symbiotically connected to earth's rhythms and cycles. He lived harmoniously without separation to the ebb and flow of life, to the seasons, to day and night, to darkness and light. He accepted the mysteries of life through rituals, such as shamanic or trance journeying. He understood the use of sacred postures, dances and movement that allowed him to experience life in connective ways, flowing in and out of the imaginal realm, back to matter again. To him the heavens and earth were connected through the imagined constructs for the creation stories he told and the mystical journeys he traversed, experiencing the interconnectivity of all of life.

Great Mother Earth was viewed as being all-inclusive, as she was the primal vessel that contained all things. She was honored and respected because she was seen as a living, sentient being who loved all that came to live upon her. She emanated all life as her body nourished her family of humankind through her gifts of sustenance, shelter and transformation from birth to death, as man returned to her earthly womb.

In the beginning, women were the keepers of the rituals within their deliberate movements of dance that told their magical stories of alignment with the cycles of nature, thus with Great Mother Earth.

Women came to represent the immortalization of the Great Mother Earth. They reflected this power, as they imparted the wisdom they knew about their world through the movement of their hips. They celebrated their connection to life and cycles found only in the hips of a woman. With connection, understanding and meaning comes empowerment.

As a woman danced from her hips, she emulated life. Her body was magically rhythmic, paralleling the flow of the moon phases, reflecting fertility, while she offered life from her hips. The lunar phases in the night sky aligned with a woman's changes in her own body each lunar month, as seen in the light giving stages of the moon waxing into its fullness and then waning, dying in its darkness again. Woman was associated with the moon and this dark-scape where the moon held domain during the time of her menses. When the moon died and the sky was dark, a woman withdrew from her community and spent time with her internal wisdom as she renewed herself. When the moon died to darkness, resurrecting on the third day, woman also resurrected in her physical and spiritual renewal and returned to her community. Many of the death, resurrection and renewal stories we know today began with these ancient blood mysteries of woman.

Women were revered during these times since the changes in her body mirrored the pulse of Mother Earth and the creation stories they told. Thus, women were associated with the Goddess who gives life, venerating the celebration of her body in its entirety and wholeness. After all, it was the woman's body that gave birth to man over and over again with each new gestation, each new cycle. This early concept of female experience that became the feminine principle was that of a nature-based, interconnected existence for all creation, both in life and in death.

The Banished Feminine

The Goddess based cultures were prominent until the patriarchal religions and their precursors silenced them. With the rise of sun worship under a male priesthood, the much earlier reverence for the moon and her priestess was washed away by a gradual change in kingship systems, going from matrilineal to patrilineal descent. So, along with the fall in Goddess worship came more wars, crimes and tyrannous rulers. The pillage of the Great Mother Earth and the rape of the Sacred Goddess were underway.

As the female body fell from acceptance and grace, so did the value of the feminine principle once highly regarded in the Goddess cultures. Woman, who once represented the pulse of life and the blood that forms humanity, was viewed as a threat. Woman and the moon came to represent all things wicked, foreboding and dark. Within the darkness, all kinds of imagined fears can surface, and man fell prey to his fears. Unable to reconcile his fears, he pointed the finger at her. After all, she was the other half of humanity that was shrouded in powerful mysteries. She emerged as the keeper of life-affirming rituals, the healer with concoctions, the original prophetess of the oracle, the residing priestess of temples and the providing vessel, bringing life into the world. As man gained power over woman and the masculine became divine, female divinity became less and less acknowledged. The dominating male energy of humanity wanted to control all of this for himself and wanted that power he saw in woman. So, he staked claim over all, degrading woman as a mere subordinate minion and property of man. Woman became known as the lessor of the human species.

In the beginning, our ancient female ancestors were not cut off from their waist down as many of us have become within our own time and our own culture. It was a gradual progression through the millenniums for women to find themselves fully within this disembodied and disrespectful view for their bodies. In modern society, this hate starts at the waist and includes all that is beneath. We abhor our waist, our stomachs, our hips and our buttocks. (Although, in recent years, we are bringing booty back!) Since the rise of the patriarch and fall of the matriarch, this part of a woman's body has been hidden, robed, clothed, desecrated, denigrated, sewed up, cut off, chastised, shut down and locked up during what our history books would call, the "civilized society." Yet, the so-called "primitive cultures" of ancient times didn't create confusion over the body and instead honored the lower half of the body—the life-providing vessel.

Now we live from our chests up and go about life leading from our heads, our thoughts and our minds. This way of going about life is attributed to the masculine principle, which is experienced as action, pursuing, persuading and competing. These are great qualities to host when they are experienced alongside the feminine principle of reception, allowing, trusting and cooperating. When the interplay of the masculine and feminine principles within ourselves is out of balance, our cultures, our societies, our governments and our nations, we experience disharmony, destruction and desecration. Within our history we can revisit the ramifications of this lack of respect for these feminine energies. The global torturing, maiming and killing of women, resulted because of sheer ignorance and fear-based assumptions about women. In our current world, we still find this imbalance, this symptom, exhibited in the examples of global genocides, inhumane treatment of animals and the lack of respect for our natural resources, to name a few.

The overwhelming results of the banishment of the feminine principle within our personal lives, contributes to the disconnection from our bodies, from our emotions and from our imaginal undertakings. In the extremity of this regime, we treat our bodies as mechanistic—just a form in which we are stuck. We pop an endless stream of pills and substances without regard to their effects on our entire system. We feed it and put anything into it without worry of the consequences and nourishment that our bodies require. We cut parts out without concern how the body might miss the pieces extracted from it. We sweep our feelings, thoughts and internal musings under the carpet to escape our emotions. We fear expression of that part of ourselves that wants to venture into the unknown. We've been taught and told (masculine principle) to not explore such feelings, holistic understandings and musings (feminine principle) because they are not considered being of "reality."

Every now and then, we may cycle back to our center body and our heart space, but it is often too sporadic. When we do cycle back to our heart center, we begin to come back in touch with these banished feminine principles dissected from humanity's experience. As modern as we want to believe we are, there is still this huge proverbial, elephant sitting in the middle of society. This elephant looming around is the real disconnect we have with the feminine energies, thus the dark, the unknown, the mysterious and the imaginal realms. We have been spoon-fed what we are to believe and to know by various institutions, including governments, religions, schools and the media. Information is handed down to us and no longer are we taught to question these basic premises that provide us with a false sense of security, but structure nonetheless, within our boxed-in worlds.

Now we find ourselves currently within a half world that is impervious and unconscious to the repression of all things that are perceived as coming from the darkness—from out of the once sacred lunar space of the Divine Feminine. We forget that this is her domain and was once sacred and life affirming. Instead we scare ourselves with stories and myths about what lurks within the darkness. No longer do we see this as the space from which all of creation emanated. The bogeyman, demonic entities and fright-producing creatures live in the dark now. Quite possibly these legends and lore have been passed down through the millenniums after the desecration of the Goddess cultures by the patriarchal religions and remain intact to keep us from venturing into the dark. For it is within the darkness and mysterious places where true primordial power can be found. This is the power that is found within those banished places that connects us to the Wisdom of the Ages. By falling prey to such unfounded myths, we must ask ourselves, does this keep us from knowing the power found within the darkness where life starts and its association with the Lunar Goddess? Does this keep the power of the Great Goddess—the Divine Feminine—out of our reach and instead, locked within our psyches? By keeping the feminine banished, the entirety of humanity loses.

The Lonely Masculine

The masculine principle within you and within the collective unconsciousness of humanity deeply misses his consort—the feminine principle—when she is banished to the Underworld. By himself, the King exists as only one half of the equation to your wholeness. Without his partner, his sacred counterpart the Queen, he is lost. The King's heart aches for the return of his Queen. He has become too lofty without her grounding energy. He desires and needs her in order to continue his long and healthy existence and needs her to get his feet back on solid ground.

The active masculine principle needs the counterbalance of his receptive feminine principle. Together they work in unison, striving to balance their energies. Without each other they are not as effective. There is only so much the masculine energies are capable of doing without the flip side of the active energies, which is the receptive side of the feminine energies. Once you plant a garden (masculine energy), you must allow the seeds to germinate (feminine energy.) You wouldn't pull the seeds out of the earth and check on them every day (masculine energy.) Instead, you would have patience and allow nature (feminine energy) to do its work. Without her passion of the soul, he cannot reign as the King whose spirit seeks unifying the principles within. The King is committed to knowing these higher truths and, ultimately, he is committed to living in truth.

Archetypal Descent Story

Inanna/Ishtar

There is a story I first heard, while working on my master's degree studies in Archetypal Art Therapy at the University of New Mexico in the late '80s. This program was eclectic and avant-garde, taking us on a transformative journey into the mythopoeic realm where the soul resides. Definitely not the typical therapy program based only on clinical diagnostics and interpretations; instead, we dove deeply into the mythological and archetypal realms that comprise human experience, in addition to learning the necessary clinical skills for practice.

One of my memorable classes explored concepts of Jungian Psychology found within the mythologies of antiquity that still resonate within our modern world. This class fully spoke to me about the revealing journey we will take when we are forced to enter the muck, the quagmire and ugly parts of our life. These events shake us to our core. We can fight them or try to ignore them, but we will most definitely do so at the expense of worsening the pain. On the other hand, we can realize that we are not broken and don't require fixing, that life is truly messy and we just need to roll up our sleeves and participate.

This poetic story that deeply resonated with me, tells the Sumerian myth known as "The Descent of Inanna." This story was written on clay tablets dating back to at least the third millennium BCE, but scholars suspect they are much older than that. There are two later Akkadian versions of the same story with this same Queen, the Queen of Heaven and Earth, but is known as "Ishtar's Descent."

In the Sumerian writing, Inanna decides to venture into the Underworld to be in attendance at the funeral of her dark sister's husband. (Note: In another version, Ishtar is tricked by her sister to enter the Underworld.) Her sister Erishkigal is known as the Queen of the Great Below and expects Inanna to be treated with respect to the same laws anyone else would be, who enters into her kingdom. This means that Inanna would be brought to the Dark Queen "naked and bowed low." As Inanna makes her descent into the underworld, ghoulish gatekeepers strip her of her clothing, piece by piece, until she was left naked, vulnerable and dying in front of her dark sister. Erishkigal hangs Inanna's corpse on a meat hook to rot and die. After three days have passed and Inanna has not made it back to the Upperworld, Inanna's female trusted executive, Nishubur, appeals to the gods for help to secure her release. Most of the gods would not interfere, but Enki the god of waters and wisdom helps rescue Inanna. Once Inanna is removed from the hook, she reclaims the parts of herself that were stripped from her, as she ascends back to the Upperworld. However, Inanna is not off the hook yet! She must send a substitute in her replacement. Although she tries to send her consort, Dumuzi, who sits there fat, dumb and unaffected—enjoying his throne—he flees instead and his sister, Geshtinanna, takes his place. Inanna decrees that she and Geshtinanna will share the fate and reside in the Underworld for half a year each.

Now, does this story sound familiar? We have heard this story told many times in slightly varying degrees within various mythologies belonging to other cultures. One of the most famous renditions from the western world is the Greek story of Demeter and Persephone. In this story the daughter, Persephone, was given to

Hades for half the year and then allowed to live in the Upperworld for the remaining half. This story helps explain the cyclical changes in the seasons from when she descends in fall and the land moves into death and back to spring when she ascends and the land once again blooms in fertility.

The Inanna-Ishtar story created such a huge impact within my psyche. It reminded me of life's natural processes; all matter decays, submits and then dies. Yet, all matter is reborn again, but this time in its new form with new knowledge. I have learned from the Great Oracle, when a person or animal dies, it sheds its carcass and steps into its new soul body, but first it makes the descent from light (heaven) to corporeal matter (earth) to return and recycle to that place of light again. The planet Venus, associated with Inanna-Ishtar, also known as the evening and morning star, is one of the brightest heavenly bodies seen in the night sky. Venus, in her incarnation as the evening star, cycles to her death in the night sky, vanishing from sight for many days into the Underworld. She resurrects into her new life, as the morning star and can be seen low along the horizon where she ascends to her apex to repeat her allotted journey of death and rebirth for eternity.

This journey is not without sacrifice and not without growth. As found in Inanna's story, she sacrifices her current identity to reclaim what lies dormant within herself, within her Underworld. For her atonement, she reclaims a deep feminine wisdom. She is open to experiencing the essence of the human soul in all of its facets, from the aspects we think we know, to the aspects from which we are disengaged. For it is within such depths that we are shown a sense of cosmic unity and the process for obtaining balance that leads to true self-empowerment, found only within these dark and mystical realms of the journey. This descent into the Underworld, the Innerworld, has always been the initiation goal of the mystery schools, the psychotherapeutic process and the work within the magical traditions of altered states of awareness. Connecting with these inner realms requires the sacrifice of the Upperworld Self for the sake of regaining rebirth within a deeper, resonant awareness. We need our dark sister, Queen of the Underworld. She has much to share with us once we venture forth to experience and retrieve cosmic powers that have long been repressed. In this interplay, we unite the Above and Below into a new evolutionary pattern of being.

Here it is twenty-six years later and I can still recite the story and remember all of those Sumerian names, which definitely are not common to our western culture's Greek and Roman heritage. The story of Inanna felt like my first induction into a society of heroines who take a fall, as an example to others, and will inevitably encounter their personal trying experience, while also reemerging. Unveiling ourselves is part of the preparatory process of remembering our humility and vulnerability, whereas undergoing a descent is the initiation.

Meeting the Queen of Heaven

I met an embodied Inanna-Ishtar, Queen of Heaven, in the mid '90s while living in Portland, Oregon. I was consumed with studying and teaching belly dance, providing workshops to women and attending Jungian dream groups. During that time, I was writing my first book, *The Spirit of Creativity: Embodying Your Soul's Passion* with the help of my spirit friends. Working with the Great Oracle was a weekly event and quite often others joined us in our Message Circles.

Having just moved to Portland several months earlier, I was reaching out, meeting and making friends with other "seekers" within the community. I became acquainted with a couple of women who worked at my neighborhood's workout facility. Through conversation, I shared with them that I was performing sacred belly dance at an event that week and I invited them to attend. One of the gals came to watch the performance of my rhythmic, tribal sword dance. Upon completion of my dance, she bee-lined directly to me, excited to tell me just how mesmerized she was by this dance. She told me that my dance transported her back in time to the memory of a woman, I just "had to meet," who danced with the same energy, focus and awareness that she claimed I exuded. The next day at the work out facility, she gave me this woman's name along with a phone number. I saw her one more time and as easily as she had shown up within my life, she was gone. She left her job unexpectedly without any forwarding information. My interaction with her was merely a week. However, I placed a call to Juana Ukolov, the woman I was to meet.

One call became a few calls. The phone conversations that ensued were mind-blowing. We spoke the same language about the underlying powers of sacred belly dance. We discussed a "deepening" of the movements that unlocks the intrinsic factor of empowerment found within this ancient dance. We both understood how the dance moved us into realms of the unseen and into cosmic powers of transformation. Juana was looking for a way to share this wisdom with others. To me, this dance was a dance of inner strength and beauty—a pathway connecting me, the dancer, into the archetypal energies spanning back into my ancestors of antiquity, who also danced. I had always believed this about this specific dance and was beginning to explore the affects these rhythmic and geometric movements had on me emotionally, physically and spiritually. I knew that this was not kid's play or a "hoochie coochie" dance. There we were in conversation and Juana verbalized the exact sentiments I was beginning to realize myself. She spoke about the Goddess, meeting the Goddess and how she wanted to help others do the same through the disciplined study of the dance. Juana invited me to visit her at her studio the following week, where she was working with two other women and teaching them about the Goddess and the spiritual movements of this sacred dance.

I arrived on the planned evening and was greeted at the front door by Juana, but asked to turn around and go up the outside stairs that lead to a room above her garage. I thought to myself, what kind of deal is this, perhaps a speak-easy? Maybe I will need a special knock to enter. So, up the stairs I went and Juana opened the door to the most amazingly beautiful temple of a dance studio. Wow! The space was open and huge, lined with mirrors and decorated with colorful tapestries, cloths, tunics and veils. In a corner sat an old record player along with doumbeks, books, LPs and other decorative items that seemed to convey; you have just crossed the threshold into a timeless realm that is a safe and sacred space. A gorgeous glass window magnificently filled an a-frame shape that outlined the outdoor view of the majestic mountains, transforming that space into a holy temple. Whoa! She asked me to remove my shoes and to sit in the sitting area, which was at the side of the dance floor. The other two ladies arrived and our conversation of the evening reiterated much of what Juana and I had already discussed via our phone calls. After some time, we put music on and we danced in a circle. Seeing that I knew how to dance, she invited me to dance for the others.

After visiting with Juana for several weeks, the other two ladies disappeared from the group and that's when Juana and I decided we needed to teach this work together. We formed a mentor-student relationship at first, where she would speak; I would write and then formulate our class curriculum based upon her teachings and upon my studies of sacred geometry and ancient women cultures. Later our relationship became one of colleagues. We were both thrilled to have each other because we understood and shared a common love for this dance, while seeking greater truths found within the secrets of this art form. We would meet every week to communicate this information with each other. She would discuss her vast experiences as a sacred dance teacher: her studies, travels and teachings within this work. I would adapt her lessons each week to my personal studies and practice of this dance. I took notes and was tasked with communicating the teachings into lesson plans and handouts for our students in each class. Our initial class quickly grew into two classes, followed by three classes at the end of our first year working together.

Our conversations swirled and spiraled us both into the depths of knowledge similar to the messages and inspiration I was receiving from the Great Oracle. After several weeks of our exciting, evolutionary discussions that spiraled us into other dimensions of thinking and feeling, Juana was ready to let me in on her secret. I was not too surprised that she had something to tell me that she rarely shared with others. This secret held the experience that changed her life in immeasurable ways.

Juana shared with me that her health took a turn for the worse and she fell ill in the spring of 1982. She felt like she was losing her mind when she became mentally detached from her family to the point of not recognizing them in the photographs she had on her desk at work. Specialists and doctors told her she was suffering from fibromyalgia. Every joint in her body ached severely; she was suffering great mental anguish and was unable to sleep for two months. Then, one day in her dance studio, while laying flat on her back feeling immense pain, she felt a presence enter the room. She looked around, but no one was there. Juana felt a familiarity with this presence, as she felt this before when she was dancing her sacred dance. This presence literally pushed down momentarily upon Juana's body with intense pressure and then it began to subside. As it lessened, the excruciating pain in her body released and she was able to get up. She explained to me that it felt like she was dying during those months of intense pain and could look back on it now as a period of dying to her old Self. When Juana surrendered to the pain and the presence, it lifted and she felt like it was an initiation into her Divine Feminine Self.

This healing event commenced multiple visitations of the Goddesses from varying traditions and cultures, literally visiting her in perceptible forms within the sanctum of her dance studio. She spent weeks there recuperating and one by one, they all came to her and shared information with her about the Divine Feminine and her sacred dance. She described being fully conscious, while writing down everything they told her in the moment. The very first goddess that came to her told Juana that Juana was "of Her" and shared the same name. This goddess was none other than my favorite Sumerian Queen, Inanna/Ishtar! Juana was amazed to learn, but not fully surprised, that I knew all about this Queen of Heaven. It was synchronicity at play. It made total sense why I would be in my Center and spiral into levels of sacred knowledge, while in her presence—the presence of Juana and Inanna/Ishtar, Queen of Heaven. I was now communing with my favorite Queen, all because of the woman I barely knew who trusted her intuition to bring Juana and me together. It was divinely inspired.

When Juana resurrected back to her life from her descent, death and renewal, she was different. Juana clarified this by sharing what she had written about the experience:

> I experienced the Hieros Gamos, which is a true balance of masculine and feminine energies within. This is very hard to describe. Circumstances were created and other people were involved, providing deeply personal messages, as if they had been sent from above. These people and events came and went so fast. Even though I experienced the profoundly spiritual and emotionally charged inner events, no one else was aware that this was even occurring. Some things that occurred were so peculiar that I can't repeat them lest I sound crazy. I felt a literal, internal implosion that 'emptied' me—I could relate to the eruption of Mt. St. Helens, which had erupted during that time! I finally could comprehend what the Eleusinian mysteries meant. They experienced things that changed their lives so profoundly; the initiate could never go back.

The truth is these events are mysteries, which are meant to be known, but impossible to explain. As with any overwhelming experience, they have to be experienced. These experiences initiate and inform you, but you are unable to explain them in a language that is insufficient for describing them. I'm afraid these words fall flat since these experiences are emotional, spiritual and even physical in incredible proportions. The impact, which is full and rich, is not found in words. This experience is a new way of learning for us. Instead YOU BECOME IT; IT'S WHO YOU NOW ARE! Becoming the experience causes you to know from feeling such depth and breadth. I am often asked, 'Do you believe in this or that?' There is no longer a 'believing in.' YOU KNOW without question, undeniably the truth, because your whole body is involved in that experience. Not a product of your mind or head. It is pure feeling and life is fully different now. It belongs to you. You ARE it!

Inanna/Ishtar gave Juana a gift. The gift she gave Juana is called the Gifts of the Goddess and it's a dance, yet it's also a mantra with hand movements. This mantra is to be taught to all women and men pursuing the balance of the Divine Masculine and Feminine Principles within. After hearing her story, I was in a state of wonderment, curious if for a moment I had fallen into a wormhole of the twilight zone. What was going on? Juana insisted that I sit and watch her perform the dance of Inanna/Ishtar, while she presented the Gifts of the Goddess to me. Clothed in magnificent regalia, I watched as she (Juana/Inanna/Ishtar) meticulously danced in the most mesmerizing manner, undulating deep movements from within her core, while presenting them to each of the four corners in repetition. I could see the movements that gave (masculine) and the movements that received (feminine.) It was a dance that truly embodied a balanced and dynamic interplay of the masculine and feminine energies. Juana embodied the Hieros Gamos within her dance. She then recited the Gifts of the Goddess mantra and asked me to say it along with her. I was transported back in time to those days of the temple priestesses and I was receiving my induction.

I present you with the Gifts of the Goddess mantra:

The Gifts of the Goddess, which are

To think

To speak

To feel

And to create

The power and the strength of the Universe

To both give and to receive.

(Repeat three times.)

-Juana/Inanna, Queen of Heaven

The Gifts of the Goddess mantra became the way we opened and closed each and every class we held for our students. No matter where or for whom we taught the class, whether through a local community college, one we taught through our own advertisement within a rented space or within the sanctity of Juana's studio, we stated the mantra like clockwork. I followed Juana's lead with this because after all, she and Inanna, my favorite Queen, were now one and the same! Crazy? No, it wasn't. To know Juana and to work with Juana was certainly a gift. She was as salt of the earth as one can get, coming from Montana and teaching herself to tan a deer hide to being as diverse as one becomes after receiving visitations from the archetypal spiritual realm. No, after absorbing the Gifts of the Goddess dance, this didn't seem crazy to me. After all, I had always seen and experienced otherworldly forms and communicated with them regularly through my Great Oracle.

Juana and I were the perfect match to teach this spiritual movement and sacred dance form. Thirty years my senior at that time, Juana was my mentor, my sister, my colleague and my dear friend. Juana/Inanna left this world in August of 2010 and returned to her place amongst the stars. She left me with her Gifts of the Goddess. I am the custodian of it and up until now, I have only shared it within small classes of sacred dancers or within small circles of friends. Now, it is our gift to you. It is a powerful, transformative mantra originating from a celestial being. Speak it as you endeavor to find your Center between the masculine "giving" and feminine "receiving" energies.

CHAPTER VI
JOURNEY

Spiraling

Our ancestors of antiquity viewed time in circles. Circles represented the cycles of the seasons, the travels of the celestial bodies and the phases of the moon. Life worked within circles and with the invention of the wheel, life as they new it drastically changed in beneficial, evolutionary ways.

The spiral is one of the sacred forms we have in life. In fact, we live in a spiral—the galaxy with its spinning arms. You will find them in seashells, antlers, sunflowers, pine cones and many plants. We are able to hear the sounds that come to our ears, as they vibrate through our inner ear in a spiral apparatus called the cochlea. Spirals are found all over nature and express the sacred geometry found in life.

I view life in a spiral. I always have. I view this spiral, which is a circle moving around itself, but within each turn back upon itself, it moves up by another degree. It allows room for separation, thus a step away from itself. Evolution is likened to the "next step" in my mind and is visualized as many concentric spirals, moving in varying directions and at varying speeds. Our energy spirals up; our energy spirals down. Our energy spirals out; our energy spirals in. Spirals represent both expansion and contraction and within either state of being, they contain movement towards and movement away from some thing at the same time. While a spiral may be in its phase of contraction, it is moving towards itself, yet away from a point outside of itself. When it is an expanding phase, it is moving further away from its center point, yet still progressing closer to a point outside of itself. In this perspective, a spiral maintains a relationship to everything else.

When you view your journey, your progression in spirals—regardless if you are going down or up—you are still moving towards the next step. The journey into and within you behaves much like this. In either direction you spiral, you traverse; thus, you will find the next step. The next step will only be presented when you have fully embraced the meaning of the current step in relationship to the holism of your life.

In other words, you must circle the wagons, a technique used during those long journeys the covered wagons made when traveling west, exploring new territory and establishing new settlements. They found in the evenings when their journey ended for the day, that if they placed their wagons in a circle, they could maintain a cohesive and strong watch over their caravan, providing for safety and protection from outside intruders. They found strength out of necessity in the circle they formed. You too will find your strength in the protective space of a spiral, encircling each step until you can embrace it, then you can trust its spiraling progression to the next step. Each new step will follow this pattern within the Underworld and the Innerworld. You will navigate the worlds through spiraling. It is within this natural spiraling rhythm, you will begin to see an "interconnected relationship" with you and all of life. While learning to notice this relationship, you can obtain a larger perspective to the enfolding and unfolding of your path—your spiraling descent into the Underworld and your spiraling ascent into the Upperworld.

Why Descend?

There are a couple of ways and reasons why one descends into the Underworld: one, you are thrown there by life or two, you choose to discover the parts of yourself that reside there. Either way, by your creations alone, you end up in the Underworld, whether it's by conscious or unconscious choice. Often you can find the descent happening automatically within a matter of moments caused by a life experience that hits you over the head and leaves you unconscious to your descent. Other times you will recognize a change within yourself that needs to happen or is naturally occurring. During these times, you will venture willingly into the Underworld. Let us examine next how we descend by distress and how we descend by delight, while exploring their subcategories of what I call the Six Big D's of descent: death, divorce, destruction, deception, desire and discovery.

Descent by Distress

The Descent of Inanna story is told to remind you that a painful (or trickster) event will take you spiraling down into a dark place where the only way out is to take it one step at a time and remerge, not as the same person you were when you fell, but instead as a newly assembled person, where life as you knew it has changed. This is your crucifixion and can become your resurrection. Jesus was an example of knowing his ability to resurrect from a descent into death. While most have been taught to believe that Jesus resurrected from a literal death, there are traditions that view his death metaphorically as a way to teach all that we must die to our false Self in order to be born into our Christ Self. During your lifetime, you very well can and most likely will experience several events of the crucifixion and resurrection theme. Learning that there is a myth, a story, that has been told for over twenty-five thousand years can help serve as a "road map," helping you negotiate those trying times and reconnect with the cosmic collective energy of those who have also traversed the journey and triumphed as the heroine and hero in their rebirth and reawakening. They survived and so can you.

What do **death**, **divorce**, **destruction** and **deception** all have in common besides being words that begin with the letter D? Quite literally, each event destroys one's dreams. They show you that something within your life has died, has changed and will no longer be the same. Dreams are smashed with these events and you are left with a big hole, a loss. The momentum of life as you knew it now feels as if it is spiraling inwards and downwards. The spiral contracts and often you will feel a sense of an implosion inside with a resulting pain felt in the heart, the solar plexus or the gut. This is your awareness spiraling into the Underworld and taking you into the Innerworld. The only healthy choice you have is to submit and go there. Remember life's natural processes of decay, submit, death, then rebirth?

Descent by Delight

There will be times within your life that you **desire** internal **discovery**. These are the other two Ds of reasons for descent. The desire to go within, to go into the Underworld and Innerworld, happens when you work on yourself. A desire for discovery typically starts with self-reflection. You recognize that there is an internal drive to learn more about yourself. The reason could be to discover untapped talents and abilities. You may choose divination tools, journaling or past life recall as pathways to tap into these inherent capabilities. Other times, involving yourself in contemplation and meditation will take you into these worlds. One of my favorite pathways to journey within is through dreaming. Your personal and message-bearing images, symbols and signs reside within your dreams. By using lucid dreaming, waking dreams and dream recall, they become direct channels to your unconscious that dwells in your Underworld. You may also end up in the descent by choosing to work with a guide, such as in shamanic journeying, psychotherapy, life coaching, consulting the Great Oracle, hypnosis or movement meditation.

There are many paths to take that will spiral you into other levels of awareness and consciousness, but they will all lead you back to your Inner Self. The Alchemists and the initiates of mystery traditions used such paths to discover their inner latent abilities for communication with the higher realms without. The truth is that no matter how you end up in the Underworld and your Innerworld, you are being asked each time by a higher guiding force to change—to transform yourself into a greater knowing of yourself. This knowing translates into an evolutionary step along your spiraling relationship to All That Is. It is within our trials, tribulations and tasks that we connect more and more with our Higher Self and back to the Source. We may not understand this or recognize it at the time, but we will eventually, when we learn to look, listen and really hear the universe communicating with us and supporting us at all times.

Relationship with Yourself

This inner journey begins when you realize that no one "out there" is going to save you, solve your problems or give you the answers. Many, erroneously want to believe that a magical relationship either with another person or with a group of people, such as that job with that perfect company, will make one's life better. When you finally realize you cannot find that perfect thing, person, event, circumstance that will save you, you start to look inside yourself. Can you be your own hero or heroine?

The most important relationship any single one of us can have is the relationship we have with ourselves, as simple as that sounds, it really couldn't be more simple than that. Yet we have made it quite complicated as we continue to search for that magic bullet—the panacea that will make our lives grand. We want someone or something to magically appear and rescue us, making us feel whole. We have believed in that fairytale to the extent of getting lost within it and searching externally everywhere for the answer, the next guru. All focus has been on the searching "out there." With this outward searching, we often find ourselves feeling empty and erroneously feeling alone by days end. We've bought into this myth that the only loving relationship we can have is with someone else, while forgetting the most important and loving relationship that one will ever have is the evolving relationship with oneself.

This relationship is the most fundamental of all relationships. Now, what does this mean? How do I have a relationship with myself? You tell yourself through logic that because you are "stuck" within your body, your relationship is sealed by this permanent fate. This is just the beginning of your budding relationship with yourself.

It is where your journey begins. When you know that you cannot escape yourself and you will always be with yourself wherever you are and wherever you go, this relationship then starts. However, just "being" in your body is only the precursor to the equation for nurturing a relationship with yourself. The remainder of this relationship is built upon the interaction with your psychical makeup. I suggest that this is the most important aspect of the relationship you can develop with yourself. It is comprised of all of those thoughts and feelings within that create your beliefs. It is the unique way you express yourself. It is all of those dreams and desires you held as a child—your magical thinking and your active imagination. It is the essence of you that knows your connection back to the stars. It is the you that strives to know more and desires to love more.

In order to develop this relationship further, you will need to descend into your inner-workings, the realm of the imaginal. You will need to allow your ego to die many deaths in order to know the uniqueness in yourself and in others. In time, the Queen of the Underworld will disrobe you and show you your true identity. When you begin to understand who you really are, you will begin to see the essence of others for what they really are as well. The relationship with yourself at these deeper levels breeds self love and love for others, for love is the path to enlightenment. Descend to find it.

Mining

I come from a patriarchal line of miners. My grandfather on my father's side of the family worked as a miner. My father spent summers between college semesters working the mines as well. They both were involved with the mines' operations, which included tending to the maintenance of the mining tools and keeping the mining operations functioning twenty-four hours a day every day of the week.

When growing up in my family we traveled around the Southwest, visiting old mining ghost towns. Many of them were the mines where my grandfather worked and occasionally where my father spent his summers in between college years. I really enjoyed the ghost part of the visits, hoping to catch a glimpse of the adventurous spirits from yesteryear. I never glimpsed a ghostly miner, but instead came away with a glimpse into how dangerous and scary the mineshafts appeared. Granted, the mines were old, obsolete and down-trodden by time when we saw them, but seeing the rusted out equipment and partly covered, great holes in the earth, definitely made this line of work appear foreboding and ominous. I couldn't help but think about the long grueling hours they kept and the dangerous line of work these miners endured day after day, regardless of a possible collapse during their shift down under. I just envisioned them going into and working their way down, one after another, into the dark hole with pick and ax, searching deeper and deeper for their buried treasures of precious minerals and valuable resources. That was their job and with that came an acceptance of their work at hand.

As you make this descent into these worlds below, not unlike those miners who descended to find the precious minerals, you too will need to accept and trust the descent. You will be equipped at each turn of the journey with tools for new ways of functioning, while you carve out your way. You can have faith that the shafts leading into your psyche are steadfast, operating continuously and supporting your descent.

Just like the miners, you are going to don your miner helmet and journey into the bowels of the Underworld and Innerworld. Although, the miners literally journeyed into their carved out bowels of the earth, you are going to immerse yourself within the crevices and depths of your personal imaginal world. No need for a pick and ax or to prod, pry and extract the precious and valuable resources. Instead, you will enter these internal caverns with your light leading the way in pursuit of your buried treasures—your most precious and valuable internal resources—and recover what has always been yours. You will follow the clues from the distant cries of the banished aspects of yourself. You will meet the underground demons and daemons and shine your light upon them.

Then you will lay down your miner helmets and learn from the underground mystics who will share with you how to work with these discovered elements within and determine ways to transform the leaden base elements into golden opportunities of integration. You will not need to pick at anything or remove the treasures; instead, you will integrate what lies dormant within. You will transmute what's leaden, painful or difficult through the faculties of your mind and through your heart center, once you face what has been buried within.

Into the darkness we go...

PART 3

THE UNDERWORLD

While common man looks to blame other people and blame fate, noble man looks for the fault within himself.

—I Ching

THE NIGREDO

To the Alchemists, the first phase of the transformation was a personal time where one immerses into the darkness of the Underworld. The initiate takes the private time to look deeply into his soul through self-reflection, while taking inventory of his unconscious shadowy projections and personas. This process is often painful and can produce melancholic feelings, depression and anxiety, while traversing this Underworld realm.

When moving about within this often dark and sometimes foreboding Underworld, you will come face to face with the stories about this place you've been told and the stories you created for yourself. Nine times out of ten, these stories exist to keep us from navigating and discovering the seat of our power. Once we can move through the layers of our personal debris, we will come to uncover this power. Since most of us are disconnected from the imaginal realm, the feminine principle of empowered vulnerability and all things related to the mysterious, including unseen forces, we may find this realm anxiety producing and emotionally latent. This is not because it is essentially something to fear, but it is often due to our lack of knowledge about this place. Again, what we don't understand, we often fear and tear asunder or avoid all together.

Within the darkness of the Nigredo, of going into your own personal darkness, you will seek self-knowledge. You confront your inner demons not by means of your intellect, but through the faculty of your emotions. It was your intellect that neatly tucked them in there. It is your feelings that will release them. When you honestly look at yourself, feelings will emerge and you will be reduced to your core, brought to your knees. There will not be an immediate solution or answer, for you will discover that the world you once knew will no longer serve you. In this space, your beliefs will break down and you will be shown new concepts and ideas. These concepts will shake your inner foundation and push the barriers of your inner walls. You will feel uncomfortable for a time as the Alchemist reports this process taking forty days until the light is discovered from within the darkness.

Forty days has symbolic significance in spiritual traditions. Moses and the ancient Hebrews wandered, Elijah fasted and Jesus was tempted in the wilderness for forty days. The Egyptian embalming procedure took forty days and Jesus' ascension occurred forty days after his resurrection. The rain fell on Noah for forty days. The planet Venus retrogrades once every eighteen months for about forty days. All of these forty-day periods seem to relate to durations of trial and being tested.

The Alchemist viewed the process of Nigredo, the darkening, in three stages: Calcination, Dissolution and Separation.

Calcination

Calcination is the first operation in the series of seven operations that comprises the work of the Alchemists. Fire and the process of burning away the repressed energies represent the first stage of the Nigredo operation known as Calcination. These repressed energies are the thoughts and emotional forces that have been stuck and repressed due to trauma, what others told you about yourself and what your ego believes to be true. However, deep down, you know these as mistruths. Through the process of Calcination, the repressed energies emerge as you experience them fully. You gain a sense of freedom from these energies as you acknowledge and express them.

Dissolution

Dissolution is the second operation in the series of seven operations that comprises the work of the Alchemists. This second operation of the Nigredo, Dissolution, is represented by the process of adding water to the ashes of what has been burned by the fires of Calcination. Thoughts, feelings, beliefs, assumptions, opinions, reactions and attitudes must be examined to determine what is based on fact or on fiction. You will review what is truly real about you and your story. This is an emotional time when you will experience anxiety, denial, fear and illusion as you look at what emerges from the once repressed energies.

Separation

Separation is the third operation in a series of seven operations that comprises the work of the Alchemists. Separation, the last operation of the Nigredo, is at hand when you can view the polar opposites in their contrast to each other. This is where you will separate the wheat from the chaff and know the difference. The energies within that were created from the self-protection mechanism of the ego are separated from the truths of who you really are. In this stage of observation you get to choose what is important for you to keep, as you see these two parts of yourself.

In order to honestly look at yourself within the Nigredo stage— within the Underworld—you must question the debilitating misconceptions about yourself in the beliefs, thoughts and feelings you harbor. Exploring dualistic deceptions in a new light will assist you through this darkness.

CHAPTER VII
THE SEEKERS

The Underworld resides at the deepest level of consciousness within our Innerworld. It is a world of the subconscious. It is that place we are often afraid to venture, for it's where we believe our inner demons and our fears are housed. Often we have created such a schism between our Outerworld and our Underworld that we become oblivious to its existence unless we get a glimpse or an experience of it in our Outerworld—our outer life. When our Underworld is left unvisited and disregarded, that obscure and dark aspect of us—the irrational aspect that evades our grasp—remains untouched and unconscious. In our fugue state to what lies beneath, we are shocked when that dismissed, dark aspect of ourselves causes havoc within our lives. The wrath from neglect is ugly and our inner demon claws its way to the surface. Even if we are not aware of its rearing head, its influence affects us nonetheless. For many individuals, these breaks are glimpses into what is stirring from deep down below and within. In extreme cases a psychotic episode can occur. When left unchecked, overwhelming panic and anxiety attacks can appear mysteriously over night. It's as if this repressed forgotten part seeks life and freedom, for within every demon exists its daemon. This suppressed demon will necessitate and push us to face the good and the evil within us, forcing us to take a stand.

The Underworld, that mysterious, dark and unpredictable place of unconsciousness within our Innerworld has been extremely misunderstood. Regurgitated and exaggerated stories about its dreaded existence have been passed down from generation to generation, often scaring the masses into avoiding it. They were and still are told that wicked and horrendous things happen in the Underworld. The stories of condemnation from an eternal, burning hell to Dante's world of a fiery Inferno, everything becomes negative that is associated with an under, below or a descent into the depths.

We have descended into the Underworld to discover what has been discarded unknowingly and banished within this crevasse. For many individuals, such a journey inward can also happen in a gradual and harmonious way, without producing any severe symptoms. Any adverse reactions, like nervousness or emotional upset are temporary, but still, adjustment periods will be required. While uncovering and overturning the hidden aspects, you may experience many regressions in this service of self-realization. Although they seem like steps backwards, they truly are not.

Predominant human nature tends to avoid and sometimes even "tear down" what we do not understand, especially when it has been steeped in fear. Although, many people held and still hold steadfast to their avoidance of this Underworld, there have been groups of mystery traditions throughout the ages who saw past the spoon-fed fears and ventured into these misunderstood realms of the Underworld, thus into their consciousness of all experiences. Instead of viewing this Underworld as the subconscious, a realm where we are unconscious, they viewed it as a type of superconscious. They welcomed this superconscious space as a realm where true knowing, thus true empowerment resides. They knew that when they ventured into this place with a purposeful intent for understanding all aspects of themselves, they knew they would in turn grow in spiritual understanding from the clarity they discovered within. They stayed focused on this vision and held it before their inner eye. This was a necessity to their descent and on many levels they greatly benefited from it, as they discovered the truth to what lies beneath.

The Gnostics

A group of such mystics who found great value in knowing one's consciousness within all realms of existence were known as the Gnostics. They were the predecessors to the early Christians and considered themselves followers of Christ. The word "gnosis" is derived from the Greek meaning, "knowing" and not to be confused with the word, "agnostic" meaning, "not knowing." To the early orthodox Christians, the Gnostics were considered heretics because of their esoteric interpretation of Jesus' teachings.

Although, beginning in the first century, the Christians burned many of the Gnostic writings about their gospels, some of their writings were preserved and discovered over the last two millennium. In 1945 a large body of the Gnostic writings, known as codices, was unearthed at Nag Hammadi in the Upper Egyptian desert in a large sealed jar that kept the papyrus manuscripts well-preserved. Many scholars suggest that these once buried manuscripts date back to the early beginnings of the Christian era, including the newly found Gospel of Thomas, predating the four traditional canonical gospels of the New Testament. This Gospel of Thomas is undoubtedly considered the most readily comprehensible of the Nag Hammadi find.

What we know about the Gnostic teachings come from not only what their adversaries wrote about them, but also from their own writings, pieced together over time. According to the Gnostics, an individual must strive towards having a direct relationship with God through the development of gnosis or knowledge, as opposed to the Orthodox Christians' path of finding salvation through the vicarious atonement of one's sins through Jesus' crucifixion. The Gnostics believed Jesus' death on the cross was a message to each one of them that personally symbolized "dying" to one's physical Self. Furthermore, Jesus' resurrection was viewed as a metaphor, teaching them to develop their direct relationship with God while they are still alive and not after physical death. Along these lines, in The Gospel of Philip, unearthed at Nag Hammadi, it reads: "Those who say they will die first and then rise are in error. If they do not first receive the resurrection while they live, when they die they will receive nothing."

The Gnostics believed that Jesus taught them to "know thyself" through the knowledge learned by attending to their inner Self, their Innerworld. In one Gnostic writing known as, Pistis Sophia, Jesus warns, yet teaches the disciples that inner truth would bring "turmoil" but this same turmoil would ultimately bring one to "astonishment." The Gnostics believed that the "kingdom of heaven" was not a literal or physical place; instead, they viewed it as an internal state of being or realization (a gnosis.) These teachings encourage man's feelings of worthiness to himself, to his God and to the creative source of his own happiness. The Gnostic teachings are concerned with the nature of illusion, the search for enlightenment through the knowledge of the divinity within and the feminine principle found in the Divine. In an excerpt from the Nag Hammadi's Gospel of Thomas, Jesus says to the disciples:

When you make the two into one, and when you make the inner like the outer and the outer like the inner, and the upper like the lower, and when you make male and female into a single one, so that the male will not be male nor the female be female, when you make eyes in place of an eye, a hand in place of a hand, a foot in place of a foot, an image in place of an image, then you will enter [the kingdom].

Although much of the Gnostics writings were destroyed and not discovered until many centuries later, their tradition survived and had a major influence upon the medieval Alchemists and their quest for the "lapis philosophorum," the Philospher's Stone. This Stone represents the purification of the soul and its union with spirit. In their private laboratories, they worked with formulas, applying various processes to base metals and turning them into gold. Some say they were not only transforming lead into gold, but were in fact, transforming their souls. The merging of the feminine and masculine essences within the metals (and within themselves) occurred, thus producing its offspring, the Lesser Stone. Once this Lesser Stone unites with the powers of the Above, it creates the Greater Stone where one is free to express the bliss of one's true presence. It is the Quintessence, supreme on all levels in which it manifests. Working with such higher truths, the Alchemists, not unlike the Gnostics, had to work under great secrecy to protect their transformative work, for the ruling religious factions considered such inner work to be blasphemous and punishable by death and obviously found such practices threatening to their ruling power.

The Hermetics

One of the oldest forms of Gnosticism is the Hermetic tradition. Hermeticism is the path that leads to gnosis, thus leads one to knowledge. It is an ancient spiritual, philosophical and magical tradition that teaches the path of spiritual growth. It is this precise path that the Alchemists were said to be embarking upon, as they transformed their souls. All Alchemists practice the Hermetic principles.

The mystery tradition of Hermeticism, ascribed by Hermes Trismegistus, "Thrice Greatest Hermes," is based on his writings that share a series of cosmological and ontological laws by which the universe operates. His writings profoundly opened the door to gnosis, which were considered the true knowledge of God, knowledge that is gained from personal acquaintance and not from the study of texts or recital of creeds and prayers. Hermes Trismegistus is his Greek name, although the Egyptians call him Thoth; it is suspected that they are one and the same. He was believed to have lived during the time of Abraham of the Old Testament, around fourteenth century BCE. There is inference that he is the reincarnation of Enoch from the Old Testament as well.

Alexander the Great, King of Macedonia, found the well-known and greatly influential Hermetic writing, known as the Emerald Tablet, within the tomb of Hermes'. The Tablet was on display in Egypt around 330 BCE, but once all of the religious zealots started another book burning phase during the fourth century CE, the Emerald Tablet was reportedly buried in the Giza plateau with hopes to protect it. To the Hermetic traditions, the Emerald Tablet was considered to hold a secret formula for transforming reality. Its principles circulated throughout various occult texts within other mystery traditions. One of its such influential maxims is, "As above, so below." This law reminds us that whatever occurs on one level, will occur on its corresponding level and that man can come to know the universe by knowing himself. The Emerald Tablet provides maxims for obtaining the unification of man with God and is the precursor to the body of work by Hermes Trismegistus known as the Corpus Hermeticum. Scholars all around the globe embraced the writings and its message, circulating copies of the Corpus in Egypt, Greece, Rome, Persia, India and Renaissance Europe. Not only did the Corpus influence these major civilizations, but also the Hermetic passages and principles were quietly integrated into many of the major religions and belief systems, influencing Paganism, Judaism, Buddhism, Islam and Christianity. The Hermetic teachings exist as the basis for all forms of mysticism and many religions to this day.

The Alchemists

Alchemy is probably most widely known as a type of medieval metachemistry, where the Alchemist applies processes and constituents, endeavoring to transform base metals, such as lead, into gold. These Alchemists approached their work as a science and an art, while cloaking it in secrecy, but following natural laws. These are the same laws that dictate the existence, the growth and the operation of the entire cosmos. Within the private Alchemists' laboratories, these laws were applied to metals, substances and processes to imitate and accelerate the process of nature through strict control of the environment. The aim was to increase the frequency and efficiency of natural cycles within a closed system of beakers, flasks, stills and alembic containers in order to create the ultimate substance, which the Alchemists called the Philosopher's Stone. These Alchemists worked to transmute the base metals into gold in pursuit of this Stone.

Another less known form of alchemy is known as Philosophical or Hermetic Alchemy. It is a philosophical and spiritual form of practice to transforms oneself. This form of alchemy is Hermetic in nature, thus helping the disciplined student discover what life is about, what is one's relationship to life and what can be done to spiritually transform one's common essence of man into the divine essence of man. He strove for clarity in his awareness and ascension into his Higher Self. However, this is only possible if one understands the true nature of man with the firm understanding that man is in essence a Divine Being.

Man is born a product of nature. Man, not unlike the rest of life forms in nature, produces a by-product known as waste. This unwanted waste is created out of the natural growth cycles that all of life adheres. Man follows similar cycles of growth where he creates unwanted waste as well as wanted creations. Yet, unlike nature, man can transform his unwanted waste into what he desires. These creations can be experienced in man as positive and negative experiences. When man utilizes his negative experiences as a way to understand what he doesn't want, instead of viewing them as "bad" and without judgment of the experience, he will be able to transition his current experiences towards balance as he strives more towards those experiences that feel good.

For the most part, we grow up in our society unaware of who we really are—our divine inheritance. The study of alchemy leads one to the discovery of the spiritual connection within oneself, with nature, with the cosmos and especially within one's relationship with the Divine. By traversing the path of alchemy, the Alchemist is able to manifest the true divine potential. One learns to transmute common, everyday nature and waste into the full divine nature that one really is.

The process of transmutation, thus transformation, consists of gaining awareness of our physical, spiritual and emotional energies as pathways to the interconnectivity with our Divine Center. When we endeavor along this process of change, we find ourselves traversing through our various layers of consciousness, emotions and thoughts while seriously taking a look at them. No longer can we blame outside influences as the creator of our negative or positive experiences. This process of awareness awakens people from their slumber of who they think they are and what they think their world is to becoming fully awake to their participation mystique with their Higher Selves and within the world of their creation. When we gain such clarity of our role in creation, we are embarking upon what is known to the Alchemists as the Great Work.

The essence of the Great Work is a personal and spiritual process that is about the purification of experience and awareness. At the basis of all spiritual practices is the purification through the understanding and transmutation of unwanted emotions and thoughts. The Alchemist takes the time to observe behaviors and follow them back to their source—willing to face the Shadow Self. The Great Work teaches how to practice this process and how to clear the mind, ultimately sharpening awareness, enabling more light of the Divine Self to shine.

When one first embarks upon the alchemical work of transformation, the process of introspection, as found in meditation, illuminates the chaotic nature that resides within. When you close your eyes and try to quiet the mind, you find your emotions, feelings, thoughts and bodily sensations popping up, swirling around your mind and distracting you from a focused, inner space. Instead, you succumb to a constant flow of random thoughts that seem to have a mind and will of its own accord. With your eyes closed and first attempts at meditation, you will find a complete mess inside. This is the unbridled chaos the Alchemists forewarned us about, but it is within this chaotic place you will be initiated into the Great Work, whereupon the cleansing and purification processes commence.

In order for the Alchemists to write about the processes they were engaging and their resulting personal experiences, they relied on creating symbols, allegorical stories and narratives. They would use images borrowed from astrology, current and ancient mythologies and symbols for compounds to express their work and internal transformations. The Alchemists could quite easily hide their truths by over complicating their writings with this symbolic language. With the rise of Christianity and its rejection of Hermetic philosophy, alchemy came under religious and political attack at various points in medieval history. Not only did they need to shield their Hermetic work and beliefs from persecution and punishment by the religious fanatics and political authorities, but they also needed to protect their knowledge and teachings from those they deemed unworthy.

The alchemical process begins and ends with what they call, "Prima Materia," the First Matter. It is the prime substance of everything in the world and of the cosmos. It is also the basic substance of our soul, the source for all transformative energy. The First Matter is born from the sacred union of the opposites within ourselves. The Emerald Tablet speaks of the archetypal Sun and Moon being the Father and Mother of everything. It is this mystical union of the Solar One Mind with the Lunar One Thing, which the Alchemists call the sacred marriage of the Sun and Moon or, respectively, the inner marriage of the King and Queen. The idea is that the Alchemist unites the above and the below within the body through their Hermetic practices. The Alchemist strives to obtain this sacred union, also known as the Hieros Gamos, by employing the spiritual practices of alchemy. This union is necessary in order to create the new change, thus the birth of the First Matter within his life. This First Matter represents a new level gained into spiritual understanding of his connection with Source and all of creation. So, metaphorically and literally, the Alchemist transmutes the First Matter as a byproduct of this newly found clarity in awareness. Literally, this means that he follows the path and processes towards enlightenment that the Emerald Tablet imparts. The Alchemist moves into higher realms of wisdom as he learns and practices the processes that assist to clear away the clutter of his mind and instead serve divine wisdom. One comes to know God through knowing one's divine essence. The Alchemist learns that one is responsible for one's thoughts and feelings, thus becomes the co-creator of the experiences the Alchemist has within the world.

C H A P T E R   V I I I
THE ILLUSIONS

Nature of Nothing

The advancement of civilization was revolutionized by technically controlling the combinations of positive and negative electronic charges, known as 1s and 0s in computer binary code. In electrical terms, the positive charge is considered the masculine polarity, whereas the negative charge is considered the feminine polarity and now also called the cathode. This relationship between masculine and feminine polarities exists within every single thing, down to the smallest known particles.

It is known in small scientific corners that these binary principles are contained within and influence how everything in the universe operates. The contrasting relationship between nothingness and "somethingness" is found within all seemingly opposite relationships, such as hot and cold, light and dark, above and below and order and disorder. These pairs of opposites are the fundamental principles of all existence and one cannot exist without the other. How else would you be able to understand one without having the other as a contrast to learn about it? For example, you wouldn't know what something is if you didn't have its contrast of nothing.

Computer binary code shows us that there is an inherent balance between the opposite forces or charges that enables its system, and for that matter, all systems to operate. This is the blue print—the base code to the entire universe—and this all-pervading principle affects everything within it. For example, when you view two opposites, they exist in a complementary balancing act within a state of neutrality; one is positive and one is negative. They cancel each other out and equal a state of nothingness, but still contain a potentiality. In their natural state of being, they are neutral and represent nothing. Once we place our attention on them, meaning is ascribed. Now, they represent something; one is considered positive (what you want) and the other is considered negative (what you don't want.)

I liken this to the nature of a Ouija Board. It is neutral by nature; it is nothing, but in a state of potentiality. Once we choose one side of the polarity to describe it—good versus evil—the Board now has meaning and is considered something. We will get that "something" that we are fixated upon. Let's say you view it as evil, then the alignment of your energy creates the fixation of evil energy towards that side of the polarity. Wherever motion and energy arrive, it must depart elsewhere. Arrival without departure is impossible. So, energy departs from the opposite polarity of "evil," which in this case is the polarity of "good" and moves towards the polarity of evil. Thus, where your fixation is aligned along the natural continuum existing between these polar opposites, you are aligning yourself and your experience with that energy. You create your own experience of evil or good and magnetize this energy to you based on where your attention (of your thoughts and feelings) is fixated.

Nature of Dualism

We've been taught an error in thinking, which leads to an error in feeling. This error, this half-truth, is so profoundly misleading that it's damaging to ourselves because it disempowers us from our creative force. It's an ultimate half-truth that keeps us segregated from the fullness of ourselves, in denial of our wholeness. And this erroneous belief keeps us locked within a cubicle of ignorance, away from the full expression of our true spirit. It keeps us separated from others and ignorant of the concept of unity.

This misconception is the belief about an existing disparity between polar opposites. Dualism teaches us that there are two opposing extremes and that one of these positions is "better" than—should be "chosen" over or should "exist" in lieu of the other. When we dig a little deeper into the polarities of opposites, we come to discover that they exist on a continuum together. The pair of opposites is really the two extremes of the same thing, but containing varying degrees between them.

Viewing these opposites as existing on a spectrum with one at each end, does allow us to differentiate energies by contrast. This is a necessary step within the evolution of consciousness. We learn what we want by knowing what we don't want. It's a reductionist way of viewing the world, seeing what we call "opposites" as existing only in their half of the part and not within the sum total of their parts. This is a stage of development that many do not get beyond, which keeps us enslaved and naïve to the wholeness of our nature and to the wholeness of our connective world.

The polarity we are taught in the Judeo-Christian view is the body's fall from grace as seen in the fall of the feminine principle. The sensuality of Eve tempts Adam with the fruit and then we spend the remainder of our lives seeking the great redemption. Our psyches are influenced by the disgrace of the tempting feminine body, whose opposite is the rational, compliant male in this story.

In dualistic thinking, everything that appears to be its opposite is pitted against the other: light versus dark, above versus below, good versus evil, heaven versus hell, and the list goes on. This thinking becomes one of exercising power over or against. The more we stay in this stage, the more we become owned by a polarization and its evil twin, zealous righteousness. This is when we actually begin to believe that if one thing is good, then it is not bad and if it is not bad, then I'm good when I'm aligned with it and others who aren't aligned with it, well, must be bad. There is no room for degrees of separation or the shades of gray. As simplistic as this sounds, think about it, this happens everyday all around us and even between nations. We become separatists and elitists, aligned with specific political platforms, religious views, communities and cultures. It's okay to belong to groups and platforms, but we only operate on a very basic, elementary level of consciousness when we judge one as good and the other as evil—one as right and the other as wrong.

The world of duality belongs to the earlier stages of child development. For example, as a child you were taught to be a good child versus a bad child, get good grades rather than bad grades and tell the truth instead of lying. You were taught there are certain absolutes in which to align yourself. During these growing years, it was important to learn about the world through positive and negative statements and experiences. After all, you were learning that there are consequences to actions, thus decisions to make that advocate a specific code of conduct in order to exist harmoniously within your family, your school and your community.

As you grow in years, but continue to maintain this child-like thinking of good versus evil, white versus black, right versus wrong, you run the possibility of not seeing the entire picture. As an adult there are new decisions to make based on new perspectives gained within the context of the ever-changing world. Absolutes may still rule certain aspects of your life, but now is the time to see the shades of gray within. Remaining in the limiting confines of dualistic thinking, you will end up gravitating to one side of the contrast at the expense of the other side. This can become dangerous when you use it as a way to judge and shun others. Know that when you judge and shun others, it is a reflection of what you have already shunned within yourself.

There is no better way that this presents itself externally within our world than in the arena of war. Many wars, if not most, are fought surface-level in the name of religion. One religious order believes that it's the right religion and the other religion is wrong. On a deeper level, we see that the excuse to fight for the right religion becomes a smoke screen to the fight for political and economic gains. Whether we always know the reasons behind the fighting and unrest between nations, at the basis of it all is the belief that we are right and they are wrong, we matter and they don't matter and we are wealthy and they are poor.

Now, realize that every time you say that you are right and they are wrong, you are good and they are bad, and that your viewpoint matters and theirs doesn't, you fall further into your isolation from others. The truth is you are more like them than you are different. Take this a step further. Let's say you do this within yourself; you judge your own experiences in this manner. You see yourself so aligned with what you believe to be good that you are unable to see the part of yourself that is not so aligned with the good. You try to escape what you haven't been able to reconcile within by aligning even further with what seems to be good, holy and righteous. Now, you become dangerous in your fanaticism as you attempt to escape every evil out there, when in actuality you are running further and further from the main evil you fear—that which dwells within.

In actuality, you unknowingly decide to cut off and cast out that part of yourself you don't want to face. These thoughts and feelings become bad, forever cast into a state of oblivion and into a dark, unconscious state. By becoming identified too closely with the light—the good and perfection—you end up creating an idealized image of yourself that is based on erroneous thinking. However, what we try to avoid within ourselves, will most certainly emerge and hit us from behind eventually.

The goal is to find balance between both the polar opposites in a zone of neutrality so you can see the opposites for what they are. When we shift into a unified approach where we can understand that the polar opposites in life and within ourselves shift and change from one side of the spectrum to the other, based on the context of a given situation and based on the shifts in our perspectives, we grow. Nothing is black and white. Life truly is about the shades in between.

This transcendent understanding promotes a profound acceptance of the universal life energy that exists as either creative or destructive, yet within the same energy continuum. Choice is what allows us to channel it as needed. This understanding allows us to know how to work with the universal life energy and use this contrast in order to co-create our lives. We must understand that we, as humans, will always experience the contrast found in polar opposites. This contrast exists for the mere purpose of showing us what each side of the continuum holds so we can determine what we want and what we do not want. Knowing that we have a choice to either create with the constructive creative energy or create with the destructive energy, gives us the power within. We can choose the creative energy, but not at the expense of denying its energetic counterpart, "destruction." As there comes a time for the necessity of utilizing the destructive aspect of creative energy for destroying and riding oneself of obsolete viewpoints, behaviors, constraints and self-imposed limitations. In order to utilize both sides of the creative force, we need to embrace the entirety of our experiences inherent in the totality of the universal life energy.

Nature of Evil

While sitting with the Great Oracle, a discussion about the nature of evil ensued. The MOON suggested to us to "fear not evil, but to understand it." She explained that evil is just the opposite of what they would call love. It is anti love; whereas God is absolute love. Evil exists as the contrast in opposition to love. We can create our experiences from evil just as simply as we can from love, but to choose love is a path of clarity. The MOON has always told us that a path of clarity is our mission in life.

Evil is an energy that only comes to life when we give it a name. When we personify and fixate upon it, we give it power. This means that as soon as we label something as "evil," we succumb to the power of the personal and collective beliefs that we ascribe to define and represent evil. In the ethereal realm where the guides exist, they do not employ the word evil. Instead they call it anti love. They see it as a choice to be anti love, thus against love and to them that just means that someone is refusing Source or turning away from it. In their realm, all choose Source. All choose love. However, they see our human struggles with understanding how our personal choices create every aspect of our lives right down to the pain we experience and to the joy we know. They recognize the resulting effects from the choices we make. They know that we have free will to choose. They remind us that we are creating our lives at every given moment. Per The MOON, "If a literal or metaphorical prison is what you want, then choose evil, thus choose anti love."

Evil becomes a projection of our own constructs of beliefs, given what we have heard about it and what we think about it. We give power to that which we believe. I do not view evil as a tangible phenomenon, but merely a projection of our own fears and destructive proclivities we harbor within. Evil is birthed from our behaviors and projections, but not as an intrinsic force by itself. It requires our moments of personal fear to manifest externally. Also, collective hype from a group of fearful people can create a mass hysteria of group fear that manifests externally to those people who participate and follow it. We choose to bring evil to life, mostly from ignorance when we view it as a force of its own creation. Evil is **NOT** separate from us; we are its creator. Evil is that personification of our personal and collective fears.

I'm certain many of you have heard about the zozo phenomenon that quite a few people reportedly encounter when using a talking board. They report a negative force coming through their boards that is demeaning and threatening in its communications, whereas others claim experiencing apparitions and poltergeist-like activity. Some even report what they believe to be negative events stemming from zozo communications that plague their life and their families.

What could be creating such negative encounters via the Board? Is it quite possible that one's unchecked negative feelings and thoughts within magnetize those forces of like energy to one's experience? Could it be possible that such negative encounters are merely a manifestation of an individual's fears about evil, displaced upon the Board? Either way you want to view it, it's often much harder for an individual to claim responsibility for the manifestation of any such negative energy. So, instead it becomes convenient and often conventionally acceptable to blame an external source for the continuation of one's fears.

Working with such a tool as a talking board, you really do need to understand how you attract like vibrations, whether these stem from your thoughts, your feelings or your beliefs. You must also understand how you project your unchecked negative stuff onto external events, including a spirit encounter. An exploration into understanding how negativity manifests, thus creating negative experiences externally is paramount when working within other dimensions. Without knowledge of these factors, these zozo encounters do become very real for each person, producing manifestations for the senses within their reality. However, it is not as if there is a living being known as zozo who exists and is waiting to possess you. No, quite the contrary, instead, zozo exists because of you and within you! It becomes a personally tailored, outward manifestation of what zozo means to a given person when and **ONLY** when thoughts and feelings are involved that create the projections or attractions about fear and evil. You choose what you want to experience, whether on a talking board or within your every day experience in life by the thoughts and feelings that reside within you.

The core commonality of people who believe they had or have a negative entity attachment—evil or demonic—have typically suffered some type of severe, deep-rooted trauma. This can stem from a history of any number of abusive behaviors where one was manipulated with shame. This can develop from a background of fear-based, fanatic religiosity where one's sense of self and spirituality was skewed. Also, this can result from one's own repression of negative and fearful emotions in order to escape emotional pain. Regardless of how this trauma originated, the energy has remained so negative and scary—locked away inside—that it's become much easier to manifest it externally (or attract it) than to own what has been repressed within. Like attracts like and if this un-checked negativity remains, well then, that's what will be created and attracted continuously.

When people choose to view these negative entities as existing outside of themselves, they come to believe that they are pawns to the experience. They do so at the expense of giving over their power to "a supposed" force acting upon them against their free will. They deny their ability to co-create their worlds. Instead they believe that by "the luck of the draw" the energies came to them and now they are here to mess with them. They have fully given their power away. What they truly fear within themselves is attracted to them in an outward manifestation that "saves" them from themselves—their own responsibility to the situation—as one more attempt at denying what lurks as "evil" or pain within.

Science is catching up to this notion—our responsibility for our reality. According to medical doctor and scientist, Robert Lanza, we exist within a biocentric universe. The premise to his theory of biocentrism is that life and biology are key components to understanding the inner-workings of the universe. This means that the universe is created by life and is not an accidental byproduct of physics. What we observe within the external world is influenced by our internal perceptions and beliefs. Thus, the world and reality we know molds around our beliefs and not the other way around. Consciousness is what allows us to interact with universal energy that exists within a state of probability. Just like the quantum physics' double slit experiment that demonstrates how the observer affects the behavior of the particle, biocentric theory states that what we observe is dependent upon the observer and not the object we are observing. So, the observer's mind is affecting energy and is connected invisibly to the particles. In other words, what we imagine becomes our reality since we are influencing the phenomenon.

Exploring the nature of evil further, EVIL is LIVE spelled backwards. A word that can be read backwards and forwards, while spelling a different word with different meanings in both directions, is known as an anadrome. In this case, when you read the word evil backwards, an entirely new word and meaning are found. Okay, so maybe you have heard this one before, but let's really explore the inherent message, the anadrome of evil, since we are exploring the nature of evil.

There are typically two viewpoints that explore this concept, one being religious in nature and the other being philosophical in nature. From the former standpoint, evil comes from dualistic thinking, viewing it as a separate force opposing good. There is good and there is bad. Good is of the light and evil is of the dark. The latter viewpoint sees evil as a warped expression since there is one creative Divine Source and from out of it everything else emanates. This one creative force exists as only good, so evil becomes an illusion we create from our thoughts and feelings when we turn away from Source.

Both views contain a portion of the truth. The religious viewpoint recognizes the dangers of evil as a separate force existing outside of us. Evil from this standpoint defines it as an external life-defeating power that brings suffering upon us—a force from without. The philosophical viewpoint that evil exists within our own beliefs and minds recognizes the need to transcend the contrast within us. Evil from this standpoint is viewed as a reflection of our own internal dualistic struggles between good and evil, failing to reconcile them within a state of neutral consciousness—a force from within. In reality, both viewpoints are admitting that there is something called evil, but from where they believe the force emanates is the difference.

That's the entire point. Evil is an energy force that resides within the destructive forces of the creative life force. It is the polar opposite of constructive creativity contained within the creative force. Within a concept, the contrast of that concept exists. This is what is shown in the Chinese symbol of the yin and the yang. The dark and the light forces exist together in complement, yet they also exist intrinsically within each other. Thus, you have the black dot inside of the white side of the yang and the white dot within the black side of the yin. This symbol is an excellent illustration how the seemingly opposing forces are contained within the whole circle they create, while existing within each other. The yin and yang forces come to know their inherent energies by contrast of a little bit of the other part within their halves, yet both come together in the totality of the symbol to represent a mutual inhabitation of the whole.

Let's learn from this interactive and complementary symbol of the Chinese yin and yang in our discussion of evil, as it is read forwards and then as it is read backwards, spelling live. Within the whole, the two words exist. Both words live within the former word, evil. Live exists as a contrast to evil and evil can exist where we live. Applying this to human life, we find that what we choose not to see within ourselves is what we truly dislike about ourselves and instead, we project it outside of ourselves. We don't want to see the side of ourselves that could do wrong and be wrong, negative and destructive and to even comprehend that we could lead ourselves to our own demise. So instead, we often find our own negative proclivities within other humans by pointing the finger elsewhere. We easily recognize it within them and whether our assessment is legitimate or not, we project these self-hidden tendencies onto others. This is evil at its finest because now we convince ourselves to believe our theory that evil is outside of ourselves. I beg to ask, who is really expressing evil notions here? Would it be the person who is condemned by becoming the target of these projections or could it quite possibly be the one who initiates these projections?

This destructive part of the creative life force that flows through everyone, expresses itself in demeaning and degrading ways when it is left unchecked. All too often the human experience of dualistic thinking lends itself to negating our specific experience or expression as being negative and unworthy. For example, behaviors such as greed, lust, anger, arrogance and deceit are viewed as negative or evil forces within ourselves we want to deny or hate. We can't stand ourselves when we behave or think in such a manner. What we don't understand about these behaviors and their resulting feelings of fear, mistrust, sadness and apathy is that these feelings are actually the destructive expressions of the creative life force. These destructive energies are the other half and the polar opposite to the constructive energies. Both are contained within the power of creation.

This creative force is a flow of infinite energy of the universal life force that exists in everything and in everyone. As just mentioned, the destructive force is contained within this creative force as well. It is just another expression of this universal force that is always flowing and always moving from one form into another. It is the dualistic nature of this force. It contains the energy of construction and of destruction, but they exist within the universe as a neutral energy that we can choose how we direct it! Once we place our judgment upon them, we move them out of a state of neutrality. We come to understand this universal force by what it does; when it's used to create it supports or when it's used to destroy it opposes.

When we deny that part of ourselves that chooses to label some of our internal thoughts and feelings as unacceptable, thus often despicable, we shut ourselves off from a resolution of these conflicting forces within to occur. We do this by shutting ourselves off from acknowledging their existence. We sweep the thoughts and feeling under the carpet and ignore their existence. Often we do this just to escape their nagging reminder of the pain we have or are experiencing. We may receive temporary relief, but what we ignore and cast into the Underworld of our unconsciousness will reside within its own fiery inferno, creating real hell for us when it rears its ugly head.

When we open ourselves to all of our expressions, feelings and thoughts about the good, bad and the ugly, we open ourselves to the entire flow of universal energy. Now, from this perspective, we can choose how we want our experiences to be. We can choose construction or destruction. There is a place for both and both can exist within neutrality without shame, blame or guilt as we acknowledge this force, but use our intent to direct it. The choice is always our own, but we can only make an aligned choice with our intentions when we see the full picture.

Nature of Co-Creation

There are two fundamental principles through which the co-creative process works. One principle "activates" through the influence of the masculine energy and the second principle "lets things happen" through the influence of the feminine energy. When we operate under a unifying belief of energies, we set the creative forces in motion, by deliberately moving in the direction of our desire; then, we are "actively doing" and aligning with the masculine principle. On the other hand, when we allow, wait and are open to receiving the desire, we are "letting things happen" and aligning with the feminine principle. These principles are meant to be complimentary to each other and when they work together harmoniously, they create a unified whole. When they are misunderstood or distorted in their relationship to each other, they create dualism. Together, they exist within every single creative act, endeavor and all of life.

As we have discussed, every individual has these two principles residing within that are not gender-specific. When you have unchecked negative emotions within, such as anger, malice, jealousy and hostility, these emotions will inversely affect the positive creations of your desire. When you don't even understand what these emotions are, they will express themselves in destructive ways to others and even towards yourself. By coming to terms with your negative and unchecked emotions first—the shadow side of your existence—you will lessen their power over you. You need to discover these emotions, see them for what they are and come to accept them.

Going one-step further, I am suggesting that you can learn to integrate the negative emotions for positive and productive creation. This act of integration is paramount along this journey of creating your desires, but you must take self-responsibility for the consequences of your own creations. This means that you don't hand it off to another person by surrendering your responsibility or blaming outside forces for the negative creations in which you find yourself. Instead, you must know that you are constantly creating your experiences by the thoughts you harbor and the emotions you feel, regardless if you think you can hide these by keeping your thoughts and emotions locked within. You may erroneously think that if you just keep them close, ignore them or not share them with anyone, they will have no effect and go away. Wrong!

Nature of the Shadow Self

The Shadow Self is a term coined by the late Austrian psychiatrist, Carl Gustav Jung. He postulated a theory of universal forces known as archetypes that are innate patterns and prototypes for human nature, residing within the realm of humanity's collective unconscious. All of experience extends from this blue print of archetypal forces. The Shadow Self is one such archetypal force, but believed to be unique to one's personal unconscious. This force is a dark side to human nature where the individual is unable to see their own deplorable and despicable thoughts, feelings and behaviors they enact and harbor within. Instead, the individual will deeply push those dark forces down into one's unconscious awareness to avoid dealing with them. They are referred to as "dark" only because they exist in an unknown state of unconsciousness to the individual. To one's ego, dealing with these seemingly deplorable forces would equate to the death of the personality and having to face one's fears of the Underworld. Yet, the deeper into oblivion one pushes these aspects down, the greater are the projections of these ostracized parts onto the external world, thus onto people, events and circumstances. One can't bare owning these so-called ugly parts, so instead, external forces are seen as being the ugly one. These external "uglies" become a mere projection of the unclaimed and most often, unconscious parts of oneself.

When one attempts to repress what is considered negative and dark inside, that source still finds its way to the surface often disguised as a false, grandiose view of oneself. We all know someone who is full of oneself! This individual will be on a crusade to stamp out all that is negative and dark "out there," while never looking at oneself. No, this person becomes self-righteous instead. On the other hand, by identifying too much with the shunned parts of oneself found hidden within the shadow, one may get lost in them and ultimately head on a downward spiral of meaninglessness. This individual will need help to see beyond the identification with what is negative and dark within. Quite possibly this individual comes from a personally degrading environment which is all this person knows. When approaching and acknowledging the shadow aspect, it is important to become aware of it, but not identify with it. Awareness will allow integration. Identification will create another type of false sense of Self.

Denying what you would call the bad things you dislike about yourself, you will be reminded of these dislikes everywhere else. You won't recognize these as your own dislikes; instead, you will see them as dislikes within your fellow humans. You will see and judge all of the same behaviors "out there" to the extent that you deny their existence within yourself. Others will be judged as the bad and evil ones when you fall too far into this trap of denying your own internal destructive forces.

When you don't claim all parts of yourself—the good, the bad and the ugly—you might as well allow others to control you. With every aspect of yourself that you choose to not know or understand, the more you will hand over your power to external influences. You willingly become a victim to these influences. When you continue to see others from the projection of your own limited and often ignorant perceptions, the locus of power is placed outside of yourself. Instead of seeing life through rose-colored glasses, you see life through jaded colored glasses. Jaded colored glasses convince you to see that person, that circumstance or that event as the source causing you to behave, feel and think a certain way. It becomes so convoluted that you don't see any other alternative than to blame them for your problems as well as your happiness! You give away your power.

We blame everyone else, as it seems like the right answer at first. After all, why would we purposely create problems within our lives? Instead, the problems must be because of them; they made us behave or feel a certain way. We become victims to the external experiences, all the while not giving ourselves any credit to the creation of these experiences in which we find ourselves. We go about living our life, while viewing ourselves as people living within a big knee jerking, reactive world. What if there is another possibility beyond living reactively? Let's imagine for a moment that another possibility does exist. Instead of looking outward for the cause, we look within for the cause.

Now, the assumption shifts to seeing ourselves as the manufacturers—the creators—of these happenings. In this possibility, we take the helm as a powerful creator, co-creating our lives, our paths and our worlds along with the universal, creative life force. We are the "imagineers," the conspirators, the directors and the actors within our self-created dramas. We create by conscious, deliberate choice and we create out of unconscious reactions to our unseen stuff. Remember that stuff we pushed way down into the deep crevices of our minds, our subconscious? We only did so out of hope so that we might gain respite from its content. Well, guess again. We never can leave it forever; it is potential energy and the energy will affect us. Instead, we must work with this energy by becoming aware of it and even more simply, transmute it from this space by a new perspective in awareness. Transmutation occurs when we direct the contrast of its experience to it. If we feel "shame" we direct its opposite of "approval" to it. Know that the universal creative force in its totality of construction or destruction will support any feeling, thought or belief we are feeling at any given moment.

You begin by meeting these typically shunned parts of yourself by welcoming them at the door and inviting them to enter. You acknowledge their existence within your life as being in service to you. After all, there is a reason for the ugly parts of yourself that are present, so appreciate their presence within your life. Inquire to their message. They always bring a message of assimilation and hope when you welcome them to step into your life. Most often, hidden treasures in the form of latent talents, abilities and inner strengths are hidden within their guise. By incorporating their messages and lessons they teach, you open to knowing more of your grandest Self. The path here is to truly know yourself—to know every bit of yourself. Yes, it's a process, but nonetheless, it's doable. If you don't embrace all aspects of yourself, you will continue to find yourself unplugged from your Higher Self, your guiding Source.

By accepting, thus welcoming all of these fragmented parts of yourself—the good, the bad and the ugly—you will grow in compassion for yourself and for others. Instead of pointing your finger at others, while projecting your shortcomings and shadow aspects onto them, you will see that others are somewhere along the path of embracing all of themselves too. The shadow lies within everyone. Acknowledging this dark part found within you is a continuous process throughout life. Others will project their stuff on you until they too learn about their Underworld and what lies beneath. As you grow and change within this understanding of your Shadow Self, others cannot help but be changed by you and the unseen energy you exude. Although this work may seem hard to do at first, perseverance will prevail. There will always be the "tests" along this path of transformation, but the tests are only for your own edification to help you gage your level of commitment to this change that is for your highest good.

Nature of a Daemon

Socrates spoke of an inner voice that guided him throughout his life, which he referred to as his daemon. Socrates himself said:

> The favor of the gods has given me a marvelous gift, which has never left me since my childhood. It is a voice which, when it makes itself heard, deters me from what I am about to do and never urges me on.

A daemon was considered a guiding spirit that could serve as an intermediary between the gods and man. The Roman god Mercury and the Greek god Hermes fulfilled this role in mythology. Plato referred to the term daimones in his writings, meaning, "knowing" or "wise." They were beneficial golden and silver spirits, residing over the air and earth. A little later in history during Greek Hellenistic times, the daemon that once inspired and guided man was now considered a lesser spirit and its fall from grace began. In the fourteenth century CE when daemon was translated from Greek to English, it was transformed into a new meaning of fiend or devil. Originally seen as a guardian angel, within time, was quickly turned into a wicked spirit, ultimately leading to the Christian view of demons.

Daemons do exist. They are everywhere within the world of computer programming. System processes that work tirelessly in the background, while performing specific chores are called daemons. You may have even received a daemon in your email inbox. When an SMTP email you sent is bounced back to you, the email message is often sent back from a header address of "mailer-daemon" at the recipient site. Next time you receive one of these, consider it in the same light as the early Greeks, a guardian angel that has flown into your email to serve and to protect you!

Meeting A Demon

In the early '90s I was working as an art psychotherapist at an inpatient psychiatric hospital in a well-known program dedicated to treating those with Dissociative Disorders. I worked as a member of the internal clinical team who treated patients with these issues. We worked with many patients who had suffered such horrific and severe cases of trauma and abuse that their only way to cope with their past experiences was by dissociating from their day to day reality. Their disorders included Post Traumatic Stress Disorder and Multiple Personality Disorder, now known as Dissociative Identity Disorder. Since my clinical work was specialized in Dissociative Disorders, I provided the art therapy groups and private sessions to assist those with finding a creative outlet as a pathway to their well-being.

Much research has been done on the efficacy of utilizing expressive modalities to help people with dissociative disorders. For example, research shows that by employing an expressive act, such as drawing, one can begin to gain a more objective perspective of their inner turmoil by placing it out there on the paper, thus removing it from oneself. By projecting one's fears and pains into the art media, they can see it from another perspective—a more bird's eye view of the issues. This act creates a safe place to express the inner "clutter and confusion" outside so the inner Self can find reprieve from it and gain perspective. The art becomes a non-threatening means for examining and cathartically releasing the build up of inner chaos and turmoil.

There was one such patient who suffered from Multiple Personality Disorder, whom I will never forget. Let's call her Maryanne, in order to protect her identity. Maryanne came from an extremely abusive upbringing, consisting of physical and sexual torture and verbal and emotional abuse. She spent most of her adult life going in and out of hospitals and treatment facilities, stemming from a long history of self-abuse, including attempted suicides. She was a cutter, meaning she would cut on her body—often quite deeply—in various inconspicuous places to release the internal pain she could not escape. She experienced many fugue states, often loosing consciousness for hours, while other parts of herself took over and placed her in compromising predicaments. Maryanne had many various "personalities" within her. Alternate personalities (alters) are created when a young child experiences severely abusive and traumatic events that are painfully hard and too much for a young child's system to comprehend. Each alter is formed out of survival for the child and each alter has their own function within the child. For example, the young child dissociates from the experience, such as sexual abuse, and another part of the personality, an alter, comes forward and takes the pain on behalf of the child. The alters establish barriers between the other alters and the main personality, the host. In a way, these barriers exist as protective functions to save the child from all of the craziness and tumultuous experiences. However, the barriers the alters once created as protection quickly become a prison, removing and disrupting one from life. The process of therapy is to help establish openness and communication within the system of alters and host.

Constantly these alternate personalities would take over Maryanne's awareness and operate in the place of her main personality, known as the "host." It was obvious when Maryanne checked out (dissociated) and another alter stepped in. Her voice, her mannerisms and the content of her expression with the art materials or the words she used would change. The various personalities emerged to present themselves to me in time only when they felt safe to do so. My work with her did not involve bringing all of the personalities forth, but instead, involved working with the host and reaching the alters that could assist Maryanne in discovering internal safety and self-nurturance. Developing internal safety is critical for the system when the negative and angry alters within wanted to come forth and hurt her.

Maryanne attended all of my group art therapy sessions and soon discovered that she was experiencing several of her alters working together as she continued to further her creative expressions with the art supplies. She found that her alternate personalities often used the art to communicate with each other and with Maryanne, the host. Sometimes, even several of her alters worked together on the same piece of artwork, alternating their time with the art materials. As they worked together harmoniously through their artwork, Maryanne began having better days with less thoughts of suicidal ideation and self harm. The art was helping her find a sense of well-being and renewed hope for her treatment. The clinical team and Maryanne agreed that she should start private art therapy sessions during the remainder of her stay at the hospital. So, Maryanne and I scheduled two private sessions a week, in addition to the group art therapy sessions she was still attending.

During our first such session, we began exploring her created images more fully than the group session permitted. We deepened into her expressed images, thus her imagination, and called upon the alters within who provided her safety. They chose to come forth and continued to draw their fears in addition to the bonds they were forming inside. The paper became their canvas of communication. The younger alters within really enjoyed this process. They could safely play with the art supplies, while learning they didn't have to keep such a tight grip on the horrific memories of abuse Maryanne (and they) suffered.

When working with this type of population and disorder, it's always important to build upon that coalition of helpful and safe alters within who can provide nurturance and care to the host. Having said that, there are also the internal alter(s) who are angry and serve as the internal bullies, causing havoc such as, suicidal attempts, the cutting, the abuse of substances, recklessness, promiscuity and a number of other self destructive acts. The hard part about working with a person who suffers such extreme cases of dissociation, is that the host, the main ego personality, will have varying degrees of amnesia and fugue states to the other alters' activities when they step forward within the personality. They often end up placing the host in compromising situations and places that end up detrimental to the person. They are destructive.

At this point during her art therapy sessions, I was building a bond of trust with Maryanne and a handful of her alters. The trust helps establish rapport with the alters and assists them with forming a coalition of security within the person. It was during the second private art therapy session that I was privileged to meet her internal persecutor. Up to this point I had not met him, but he was the main reason she ended up in the hospitals, as he was the main alter that was the must destructive to her physical body. He came forward with a deep and booming voice. He told me his name was Demon as he jumped up onto the chair, looming above me and angrily confronting me for working with the "little ones" inside and helping them. To say he was pissed is putting it lightly, but from my experience with this work, I knew, as the therapist, I could not react in fear. Demon's voice growled, sounding like the demon voice from the Exorcist movie. I stood up too and told him that it was his turn to be heard. I would listen to him, just like the others, through his marks on the paper. He told me that it was foolish (in so many clever expletives) and that he would not cooperate. It never makes sense to force an alter into cooperation when trying to gain trust and it is never wise to aggravate one of the most dangerous alters within. Instead, I thanked him for coming forward and introducing himself to me and then thanked him on behalf of Maryanne for protecting her during those scary times of her younger life when he was present. This seemed to catch him off guard and after a few more exchanges, he retreated within. Maryanne came forward with a remote feeling that Demon must have come to the session that day. Her initial demeanor of excitement at the beginning of the session quickly turned anxious at this point. We finished the session by calming her system down and assisting her with formulated plans for self-nurturing between this session and our next. I alerted the rest of the clinical team that her destructive alter came forward and to keep continuous watch over her these next couple of days. After all, the repressed and angry giant within was stirred. That session created an opening to further communicate with this destructive and angry alter. Maryanne needed this communication and cooperation between all of her alters, including Demon, in order to function outside of the hospital watch.

I knew the work was cut out for me to assist Maryanne with her inner persecutor, her inner demon. He was a big bully to the system because of the havoc he often caused to Maryanne's body, but also because his name was associated with fear. Maryanne was raised in a Catholic faith; all the while, she was regularly tormented as a young child and told how impure she was. Her abusers told her that they needed to cast the demons and the impurity out of her. The name Demon made much sense to this alter's choice of names, so I decided to research the origins of the word, demon, before our next session was to occur in two days.

No sooner than the start of our third session, Demon came through again. He was back to vocalizing he expletives and threatening harm to the host. This time, I interrupted him and bluntly told him that I would end this session and his opportunity to speak further unless he first listened to an interesting story I had to tell him that was all about demons. Apparently this worked, as he agreed to hear the story. Rules were set that he had to listen to the entire story, without interruption and then I would listen as he told me what he wanted to say. I told him the story of a special "daemon" that was once a guardian spirit and came to protect a young little girl from scary things. In the story I shared that this protector's name was originally spelled D A E M O N and had incredible powers of healing, protection and compassion. I shared that any daemon's job as a protector could be to the daemon's own detriment, but that a daemon could rejuvenate once he discovered the hidden treasure within. I told him that this strong, guardian spirit had witnessed such terrible things, but remained true to his name and his position of protector, sheltering his little friend from pain. The story lasted for at least five minutes.

As I told this story, Demon quietly sat there listening. I had his attention so I ended the story with a question. I asked him if he knew any such daemons. His response was utterly astounding and quite simply stated, "I may have been spelling my name incorrectly." As I write this and share this story with you, I still feel emotion welling up within me twenty-four years later. It is that same feeling I felt that day—in awe of a god being born! Not only did the story transmute, it shed a light on the power of perspective and possibility. Maryanne, thus Demon, were treated so recklessly during those young years as a child, she interpreted the abuse she suffered as a punishment for being a bad person. For the first time within that moment, this inner bully saw into another perspective—another possibility—for his purpose. He lessened his grip on the system.

Our sessions continued progressing forward for several more weeks until Maryanne was discharged from the hospital. I saw her a few times after her discharge, when she became a client in the hospital's outpatient dissociative group that I helped run in the evenings. Where Maryanne is today, I do not know, but I can tell you that she found hope when Demon permanently changed his name to Daemon. He signed all of his artwork under his new name and identity. The scary demon was transforming as he recognized that within every demon a daemon also exists. He now understood the power of his choice that could free him from his damnation and provide hope for other possibilities to his existence within the polarities of bad and good. That was his beginning step towards working in harmony with the other alters, thus with Maryanne, the host. This step is the groundwork needed to develop integration if full integration becomes the goal.

Within every material form, resides a spirit that sleeps, awakening to greatness when touched by the creative realm of the imaginal. Shall we stir the gods and illuminate the world within?

PART 4

THE INNERWORLD

There is nothing either good or bad, but thinking makes it so.
—William Shakespeare, Hamlet

THE ALBEDO

To the Alchemists, the second phase of the transformation was a time when a light appears within the darkness of Nigredo. This light is the insight gained, while securing a positive attitude and manner for handling the resulting turmoil the inner demons created. The initiate has discovered his inner source latent with abilities to emotionally work through the issues and havoc. He views his feelings and thoughts as allies to this process, no longer running away from them or fighting them. Instead, he finds acceptance of them and integrates their transformation into his awareness. Through observation of himself, his behaviors, thoughts and feelings, he increases his self-awareness. Knowledge is gained to find inner unity of the polarities by comprehending the reason for their contrasts. In this stage, the initiate welcomes these energies and takes action on them through the process of transmutation.

Transmutation of unwanted behaviors, thoughts and feelings occur when the opposing principle of what is causing the problem is brought forth into your awareness. This is the inner work you must do; acknowledge what you want to change about yourself, which was discovered within the recesses of your Underworld. Shine your light on what needs to be changed by bringing it to your awareness and honestly viewing it. From this place of awareness without judgment, you can transform the energy signature of it into a new and warranted energy signature. This is accomplished by focusing on an archetype that represents the principle of opposition to it. Opposing principles have the ability to provide balance. Behaviors, thoughts and feelings can now be authentically interpreted and replaced with more favorable, alternative ways of being.

The Alchemists viewed the process of the Albedo, the lightening, the white stone, in the stage known as Conjunction.

Conjunction

Conjunction is the fourth operation in a series of seven operations that comprises the work of the Alchemists. Conjunction is the only operation to the Albedo phase, but the central stage to what the Alchemists call the Great Work. During the Albedo, a light appears within and occurs at your Center—within your heart. The Alchemists know this act as the Sacred Marriage of the King and Queen within. It is this mystical union of opposing principles that transforms you towards a greater awareness of your Center—your connection to Source. This conjunction affords you your first glimpse at higher realms of existence, such as a spiritual connection. This is the opening of the heart to unconditional love of Self, of others and of Source. The more you transmute, thus purify yourself, the more you raise your vibrations and open your heart. You begin to plug in to Source.

CHAPTER IX
GOD SAVE THE QUEEN

Reclaim the Feminine Principle

Once you know you want to discover your connection to Source and plug into the socket of your Higher Self, you will first need to explore and reclaim the repressed and buried aspects of the collective and personal Divine Feminine. As I have been sharing so far, the energetic feminine qualities of intuition, connectivity, altered states, receptivity, patience and the darkness must all be welcomed back into your world.

You will enter the world of unrealized and repressed emotions and thoughts. There will come a time when your changes within will bring you new and different expressions of these once immobilized thoughts and emotions. This work will spark your interest in learning about new ideas and concepts related to spirituality, the paranormal and metaphysics. You wouldn't be reading this book if you weren't already seeking these pursuits. The more you dig into your Innerworld, the more you will notice these changes within the traditional world in which you live day to day. As you experience the gems of the Innerworld, do not be surprised if you find your Outerworld relationships starting to change as well. You may find that you have outgrown some of your current friends, social circles, career path and past times. In their place, new interests and new people will enter. It will all be perfect timing for when you allow yourself to explore and express the realm of your Innerworld, you will make new discoveries. The new discoveries will contribute to your evolution and personal growth that will be felt internally and witnessed externally. These changes will assist you in the pursuit of having conscious contact with your Higher Self, your greatest Self. Take your time, as there will be much to learn.

The Sacred Bone

We must first reclaim the Divine Feminine found within our bodies in the region of our pelvic area, which includes the pelvic girdle (the hips) and the sacrum bone. For it is within this area of our body that reproduction and fertility occur and was revered by our ancestors. Although the entire human body has been referred to as the "sacred vessel" within many cultures and traditions, the sacrum bone has been referred to as the "holy bone." The name "sacrum" comes directly from the Latin word "os sacrum," translating to "sacred bone." Further back in history, around 400 BCE the Greeks called this bone "hieron osteon," translating to "holy bone." Crossing the ocean and onto another continent where the early Mesoamerican cultures thrived, their languages contained words that refer to the sacrum as a "sacred" or "holy" bone as well, suggesting independent naming practices rather than learning about the given name by being in contact with other cultures.

We can assume that the sacrum was considered sacred and holy, perhaps due to its close proximity to the reproductive organs. After all, from out of this space arose new life. The sacrum is a hard bone that after death and the burial of a body, it is often among the very last visible remains of a body in both humans and animals, long after decomposition. Often these sacrum bones were found carved into skulls or ceremonial masks. This may suggest that these people saw a connection between the pelvic girdle and the skull—the pelvic and the head. Around various parts of the globe, there is a belief that the sacrum bone contributes to a rebirth and is therefore known as the "resurrection bone." In Mesoamerica cultures the sacrum represented a portal or doorway between the worlds. Shamans traveled between the worlds and communicated with deities through cosmic portals.

From a structural perspective, the sacrum bone is an important bone to the fulcrum for support of the torso. We sit on it and rely on it to support our torsos for extended amounts of time, which we are able to maintain without significant movement. In this sense, as it supports us, it becomes our throne. As we sit on our hips, our pelvic girdle, our sacrum, we own our thrones. This is a sacred place and you are royalty when you own the throne of your hips—your sacrum. I often tell women friends to "get your hips on and own your throne!"

An interesting point to consider is the location of the human body's center of gravity. It is different between women and men. So where do you think the center of a woman's body is located? You've got it! It is located in her hips, more precisely, at her sacrum. A man's center of gravity is within his chest. When you breathe into your hips and then connect that breath to your heart within the area of your chest, you are connecting these two centers of gravity together. (See Hips to Heart Breathing.) Thus, your breath becomes a bridge, connecting the feminine energies with the masculine energies, enabling both to join as one at the heart.

The Sacred Heart

The heart is the hardest working muscle in our body, beating about forty million times a year reaching approximately two and one half billion beats by its seventieth year. Not only does it perform this physical support for our bodies, it performs a spiritual support as well. The heart is our tuning fork, our place of transmutation and the central chakra to the rest of our energy centers located throughout our body. The heart is in the middle, which is the center chakra to the three chakras below and the three chakras above. It is where the Above meets with the Below and the Below meets with the Above. When you go to the center of the matter, the center of your emotions and the center of yourself, you will find the answer. For it is within the Center where we will find the heart of the matter. The power of transmutation resides in the heart. It is the source of our creative response to life.

Every tool we explore within this section of the Innerworld supports the expanding heart. Visualize the image of the inverted triangle (masculine) meeting with the upright triangle (feminine) within the center of your body, where your heart is located. This looks like two triangles superimposed, forming the symbol of the six-pointed star, the hexagram, known in different traditions by different names. Several names it is known by are the Star of David, the Seal of Solomon, the reconciliation of the opposites of fire and water, the Divine Union of male and female energy, the fifth element (quintessence), Nirvana, the King's Star, the Star of Creation, the Tree of Life and in three-dimensional form, the Star Tetrahedron.

Once the lofty ideals of spirit merge with the grounded ideals of matter within the heart, the feminine and masculine come together in their sacred embrace. They become lovers within your body, encompassing the fullness of the upper chakras with that of the lower chakras. The heart knows and integrates what the truth is when bringing all matters of concern to this place of Center, not unlike the Egyptian Goddess, Maat, who weighs the heart on a scale against her white feather. She does not assign judgment or reward for how life has been practiced; instead, she looks for balance. When there is balance, the process is complete. When there is not balance, the process continues.

As you endeavor to spend more time within your heart center, you will learn to trust the knowledge and wisdom that are at home there. Interesting enough, neurocardiologists and many other scientists believe the heart has a brain of its own. Its elaborate circuitry and network is similar, yet it's enabled to function independently from the cranial brain and nervous system. This is why heart transplants work. The heart's brain can learn, remember, feel and sense. At the Institute of HeartMath they are researching the "brain in the heart" and learning how the heart brain communicates with the cranial brain. Their studies show that not only does the heart's brain process information, but communicates its input, neurologically, biochemically, biophysically and energetically to the cranial brain. They found the heart's electromagnetic field to be the most powerful field created by the body, being five thousand times stronger than the field produced from the cranial brain. They found the heart's electromagnetic field not only permeates throughout our bodies, but also radiates outside of us and can be measured up to eight to ten feet away. Their research indicates that not only can the cranial brain detect this energy field and respond to it, but others around us can too.

Hips to Heart Breathing

Understand that when you "own your throne," you are honoring the region of your hips and all it represents. You are honoring the "holy bone," the cosmic portal into other realms and the place of birth and renewal. Likewise, when you relax into the wisdom of your heart, you are tapping into the seat of your soul, your Center.

Desiring to connect these two powerful centers of the hips and heart within my body, I developed a breathing exercise to accomplish this dynamic connection. This special type of breathing exercise developed out of my work with the Great Oracle. I not only use it when working with the Great Oracle, I have also incorporated it into my personal meditations, journaling sessions and all other spiritual pursuits. I even use it whenever I need that little extra boost of confidence and guidance. Once I began experiencing the results of this type of connective breathing, I taught it to the other Great Oracle Operators and all others attending the sessions. This technique quickly grounds and relaxes the breather by promoting an opening of the heart chakra for authentic and receptive communication. Now, I use this technique within any given day, within any moment of time that I want to make sure I am in a coherent connection between the throne of my holy sacrum and my open heart. This is a channel I purposely create, raising the energy from my sacral chakra at the base of my spine (the sacrum) to the Center place of my being—my receptive heart chakra. From there it radiates out.

I suggest that you not only implement this meditative breathing into your Great Oracle sessions, but into any type of spirit communication you do. In fact it has so profoundly influenced me that it is the cornerstone and jumping off place for working with all of the tools and techniques found within this section. Use this technique as your breath work, preparing for a Great Oracle session. Have the other participants and Board Operators do the same. Take your time until you feel that everyone within the session has reached a place of connection and coherence between their hips and hearts. (To learn more about how to work with the Great Oracle, a talking board, read my book: *The Spirits of Ouija: Four Decades of Communication.*)

Here is the breathing technique explained in the form of a guided meditation:

> As you sit in your space, preparing for your spiritual work, bring your attention to your breath. Take your breath into a longer and a slower breathing pattern and as you do so, imagine yourself dropping your focus, your awareness, your breath into the fullness of your sacrum, your pelvis, your hips. Breathe into this space with your long, methodical breaths to drop all of your weight into this location, allowing your shoulders and rib cage to drop as well. Breathe and center into the seat of your hips, your throne. Once you feel relaxed within this space, bring the awareness of your breath into your chest, into your heart area. All the while, your hips remain centered and grounded in your throne. Now, breathe out of your heart as if your heart can breathe. As it breathes, it opens, and as it opens, it relaxes.

Continue breathing into this space and relaxing into the expansion within yourself within your heart space. Now, imagine the feeling of love breathing into this space with each in-breath and then imagine the same feeling emanating out with each out-breath. Relax. Breathe. Feel. Expand. Allow.

You only need to take a couple of minutes with this breathing exercise. Over time and with consistent practice and repetition, you may start to feel a warm vibration arise from within your body, intensifying within the space of your heart. This is all good. This is your intuitive heart, opening and expanding within your conscious awareness. It is this type of expansive energy and open awareness you will bring into your work with this section's tools and it is this awareness I encourage you to further develop within each technique. Once centered within your heart space, you are ready to deepen your work with the tools and techniques for accessing other realms of consciousness and connecting with your Higher Self.

Reclaim the Imaginal Realm

The faculty of the imagination exists within the imaginal realm of the universal, collective consciousness. This realm is much more comprehensive than and more expansive than the realm of our mind. Imagination is our ability to glimpse reality in an unprecedented manner. The imaginal realm is as real as the reality in which we navigate and move our physical bodies. It is just as real to the child speaking with her "special friend," even if no one else can see or experience this friend too. Within our minds we enter the imaginal undertakings. We can go anywhere, we can be anything and we can create anything, while entertaining ourselves for hours on end. Who is to say that when we are within this inner space that is not a real existence? It is just as real as the dreamscape we enter every night when we go to sleep. It is the realm where our ideas are created and are translated into images, such as symbols, words and thoughts, enabling us to communicate these imaginings with others. I'm suggesting that we value the faculty of imagination and the imaginal realm as much as we value our ability to communicate, to think, to reason and to access logic. Great inventions, artistic masterpieces and new technology start within this space. Without the faculties of our imagination, we wouldn't progress. We wouldn't exist!

The landscape of the imaginal is one of malleable potentiality, mysterious images, inner daemons and infinite creative possibilities. This landscape contains the potentiality of all endeavors and shines light upon all realities as being primarily symbolic and metaphorical. Its rich images have always been the mother of creation. All of what we call "human reality," whether it's economic, social, religious or physical is derived from psychic images, having taken shape within this imaginal realm. This realm provides the Prima Materia that is perfect for birthing and bringing forth new ideas, allowing fruition to images. It is a very real part of our existence. Yet, it can be hard to put a finger on it, as it is an illusive, mercurial landscape, shifting and changing that is home to the master, magician, Alchemist, Hermes Trismegestus.

The Alchemists were very familiar with this powerful realm. They encoded their formulas in paradoxical equations comprised of images, symbols and obscure messages, which find their metaphorical meaning within the imaginal realm. Following in Hermes footsteps, they were magicians of this realm—I-MAGI-NATION—I am a magi of my world. They knew they were the magical craftsmen of their time, creating their realities in the manner and form in which they wanted them to appear. They were known for their ability to extend their longevity and they were known for their ability to create gold. They were known for their ability to transcend the time and space continuum and some were even known to bilocate. Not only were they magicians of imagination, they were the wise kings, birthing the Philosopher's Stone from out of the sacred marriage of the Divine King and Divine Queen within.

The Entrance

You, as the initiate of alchemy, are called to enter the imaginal realm. Remember to use the gifts of your imagination, for your journey through the Innerworld and within your inner work requires your imaginal faculties. You are tasked with liberating the Divine Feminine, as you resurrect her domain of imagination found within yourself. You will encounter soul messages from this space. All images that emerge from within you will be highly personal and uniquely yours. If you choose to continue as an initiate of alchemy, you must learn to think and feel what those images mean to you in a personal way. Remove yourself from any intellectual interpretation or you will never penetrate the great secrets of alchemy in this manner. Pay attention, for the images and soul stories emerging serve as guideposts to your journey's progress. Observe, yet reserve judgment. Listen to their meaning, but avoid slaying the dragon too soon. For if you label the emerging images through conventions of naming or defining, you immediately kill the messages before they unfold. The ego and inner demons will attempt to trick you into controlling the process. Labeling makes the ego feel safe, but keeps you from venturing forth in pursuit of the Great Work. Embrace the namelessness of the images for that allows them to unfold and open to their meaning at deeper levels and layers of your soul's inner sanctum. Be prepared. What may appear at first glance to be a monster could really be a fear cloaked in its disguise. Ego is fearful and creates the image personifying the fear. Instead, allow your imaginal faculties to unfold, while embracing the image. Don't fear the false fears. Follow the image, as it will reveal the architecture of your inner landscape from where it came. Through this process with yourself, practice embracing the feminine principles, her qualities of intuition, compassion and patience. Know that this realm evolves with you as you evolve through it. The only obstacles that hold you back from your evolution on multiple levels are your limiting beliefs created by your limiting thoughts and your limiting emotions. As you grow in gnosis by remaining open to possibilities, the experience and expression of your thoughts and emotions widen, allowing you to embrace new frontiers of greater knowledge. This is the journey of the hero and heroine. Enter at your free will.

Seeking Truth

We can approach our view towards life in two fundamental ways, a dualistic approach versus a unified approach. As we explored earlier, in the dualistic viewpoint, everything is seen and experienced in terms of good versus bad, right versus wrong and the greatest of all, life versus death. Living from a dualistic point of view, holds the deeper, true Self from emerging. It keeps us away from our limitless possibilities and ultimately, our empowerment. This is because a dualistic attitude begets such thinking as "my way, the only way or the highway," keeping us narrow-minded and from finding another way to view a situation. It keeps us from a grander experience of our greater Self in all of its possibilities.

In the unified viewpoint, transcending the opposites allows new options to form, as the polar opposites are combined into a new experience within your mind and within your field of awareness. Tension and conflict cannot exist when unified. Instead, polarities work together, showing you their contrast from each so you can understand both sides. When you view them in contrast, as opposed to viewing them in opposition to each other, you get to see the polarities for what they are. In simple terms, they present their side as just a way to understand what you want and what you don't want. When either side of the contrast is not judged as being good or bad or right or wrong, you will be able to see what could work for you, pulling from both sides of the polarities. They complement each other when observed in this manner. This allows us to learn more about the world and our relationship to it.

You move past dualistic thinking, behaving and reacting when you ask yourself to find the truth in the matter. Just by having the desire and intent to find the truth, you have just opened yourself to possibly discovering a wider picture of the matter at hand. When you tell yourself that you are right and only your position can be right, then you step backwards from finding the truth, that more than likely resides somewhere in between both polarities. The idea is to find the truth between two seemingly conflicting positions that elevates your view and stance to a new platform for seeing things from a new angle. As you view life in a more explorative and alchemistic manner for finding the commonality, you grow in acceptance and tolerance of yourself and of others. This really gives you a new perspective, releasing any tension and conflict created from maintaining your stance of fixation on only one perspective.

When you are ready to move into a new platform of understanding, you must be willing to relinquish the stance that currently holds you in this space of conflict and tension within yourself or with another person. This could mean releasing a belief, a fear or a behavior. Try viewing the matter at hand in an objective and detached way as you can, allowing your intent for impartiality to provide a new viewpoint. Be patient with this process. The ego personality wants to be right at all cost, for if you admit that there possibly could be another way to view the matter or even determine that you are relinquishing your current stance completely, the ego feels like it's suffering a slow death. The unified approach is contrary to the ego's view. So, just really pay attention to this, especially when you find yourself not being able to find any compromise or understanding of another viewpoint.

Understanding will lead you to the inherent truth. This path to seeking the truth in the matter promotes freedom as you learn that the polarities are inherent in the world to teach you about flexibility, stretching you into new ways of thinking, believing and behaving. You must ask yourself, if you want to be right or if you want to know the truth. Finding the truth means becoming vulnerable to new realizations coming forth and replacing the antiquated patterns of thinking, believing and behaving that you embrace. That is scary to the ego, as it must now extend acceptance and compassion towards you, towards the newly emerging patterns and towards others in the absence of being right.

The truth will show you that the alleged problems out there are really a symbolic representation of the dualistic struggles you have within. Know that there is always so much more within you than you are currently able to access from any dualistic perspective. Call upon the truth in the matter and allow, step aside and discover an incredible force within you that will help transform the feeble mindedness and fears that once kept you from venturing beyond your one and only perspective to which you clutched so dearly. Know that only dualistic thinking keeps you from knowing your empowered Center. This empowered Center is where you create your life and your world to your liking, but only to your liking when you allow a bigger picture to emerge. This larger picture brings more possibilities to your table of creation.

Knowing the Paradox

Leaving duality behind means existing in paradox. The paradox is what remains from perceiving things in relationship to their contrast. Contrast is necessary so that we may come to understand the process of our evolution towards greater awareness in consciousness. Contrast assists us to define what is wanted, but not to the neglect or deny any side of the contrast. Wisdom is found in the containment of contrast of light and dark, masculine and feminine, mind and body and ultimately, life and death. By exploring, thus holding these opposites in contrast without judgment, we allow a new third energy to emerge. This is the transcendent function of the two opposites held in contrast by our minds, allowing a transformation into another way of thinking and feeling to occur within the deep levels of our subconscious. For within this paradoxical allowance, balance is found. Balance is the emergent new third energy from out of the old two opposing energies. This is likened to the alchemical Lesser Stone from the first round of union between opposites. The appearance of the Lesser Stone confirms the movement in the direction of finding the Philosopher's Stone.

Balance is what we must seek in order to know the whole experience of the possibilities of ourselves. Balance does not mean equal. Instead, balance relates to an awareness formed in equilibrium, an ever-changing homeostasis of our personal worlds. As we move our awareness into higher levels of consciousness, we discover that everything is neutral and has no implicit meaning. Everything exists within a balanced state. Balance is found in neutrality.

More than one thing or one side of a given situation is true at the same time. This means that all things are true, not that all things are fair, just and right; it just means that they are true. During a session while communicating with The MOON, I inquired how I could find resolution to a polarized situation I found myself within. I was on one side and "they" were on the other side of this opposition. I knew that both parties participated in creating a confrontation based in tension, whether or not any of us were consciously aware of it. We both were in this together. Yet, the pressing issue involved was that I must deal with the confrontation in a manner that maintained integrity, while not blaming the other. Instead of discussing why I created this and the lessons I could be learning from it, The MOON made a suggestion. She suggested that I find the solution for the opposition through simply finding the highest good for all. She said,

"What could you do to make both parties feel right?" I knew in my heart of hearts that they believed they were right while at the same time I believed that I was right. Instead of remaining in gridlock, The MOON suggested I could transmute the entire ordeal by simply viewing the situation from the other parties' perspective and by removing myself mentally and emotionally from the tension. At that point, I was not feeling calm. I was feeling tense. So, I went into my heart, my Center, and visualized the combative people as having a right to air what they believed to be a wrong. In that way, I could view them as doing their best, given what they knew or were told. This allowed me to understand their humanity. Then I returned to the tension that I was feeling within. I mentally held and physically felt this "tension," but welcomed its polar opposite "calmness" into my awareness. By bringing "calmness" to my attention and by internally reminding myself exactly what calm feels like, within that moment I was able to lessen the tension. I did this several more times over the following week and in no time, the tension disappeared and instead I felt a sense of calmness within and neutrality towards the situation. Even though the situation was not resolved at that time, I chose to not allow myself to be held a prisoner within this creation. I transcended it.

Oh, and by the way, the situation eventually resolved itself in my favor.

Transmuting the Paradox

Paradox is the core of wisdom, which begins within the heart. Within the logic of the heart, you can solve the meaning of the paradox. Gaining a perspective of neutrality, allows you to gain a wider perspective. You are able to view things differently; your perspective clears and you can gain clarity. Now, your mindset expands into encompassing a larger view and you actually raise your vibration.

When you experience either a state of feeling positive or one of feeling negative, you are aligned with only one side of the equation. You have interpreted it and ascribed a meaning that judges the worthiness of the experience. It's human nature to want to feel good so we often strive to obtain that as quickly as possible. When we strive for the positive charge while avoiding the negative charge, we are back to square one and relinquishing the expansion of our awareness and growth towards divine empowerment.

So instead of escaping the negative charge, bring the positive charge into the negative situation. Moving into greater levels of awareness and higher levels of vibration means introducing positive energy within the areas you feel have become negative, so you can obtain a more fluid state of balance. Once that dynamic, flowing balance is achieved, you represent a new level of neutrality—a new level of understanding.

When you come to a position of balance and the situation is neutralized, you can now raise your energy to a new platform that is beyond both polarities and reflects the true raising of frequency. In that experience you have transcended the drama or conflict and moved into a space of natural symbiosis. When you can view things from their neutrality, it's the secret to seeing things in their highest frequency—their highest good.

Techniques to Neutralize

I want to share a few techniques with you that I find helpful to use within different situations when balance is needed. Know that you are the Alchemist of your life, transmuting the leaden circumstances, thus transforming your experiences in golden, evolutionary ways.

The Power of Appreciation

How often have you found yourself in a situation where all you see is the negativity and the bad? In extreme cases, you find yourself obsessively wrapped up in ruminating over and over about how terrible it is or how much you dislike something or someone. It consumes your hours, your days and sometimes the years. Every time you think about it, you feel downright crappy, while other times you feel mad as hell. It can become a downward spiral of constant, negative inner chatter about the situation, thing, event or person. In your mind, it's not getting resolved and it probably won't change for the better on its own accord.

Here is a technique I use when I find myself mulling over something with disdain. I keep a little notebook that I call my Aspects of Appreciation. In this book, I take a topic that is extremely frustrating and give it a name. For example, let's say that you are struggling with the way another person has been treating you at work. This person's behavior towards you is condescending and exceptionally demanding. No one seems to want to do anything about it, however you can, and you can do it in a very calm and energetic way. Let's give this person a name and call him Harold. Now you and Harold have to work together, including daily interactions. He continues to demean you, making cutting comments. You are so frustrated and are beginning to fret each day you go to work, hoping he'll move to another division within the company or even get fired. Feeling this way is certainly not conducive to productivity at work, but it is conducive to practicing this technique and readjusting your creation.

Okay, so back to the little notebook. You give this situation a name and write on a page, "Things I can appreciate about Harold." What? I know; it sounds hard to think of any, but wait a moment in silence for at least one thing to come to mind. So, maybe you can appreciate his shoes. That's it. He wears nice shoes. Write this down. Now, think of the next thing you can appreciate about Harold. You dig deeply and muster one up; you do "kind of sort of" like the way he keeps his cubicle organized. Write that down. Write as many appreciations as you can, but you must write at least one. This one thing will be the beginning of shifting the energy between the two of you. Every time you find yourself consumed with the negative, intense feelings you feel about him, find something else to appreciate about him and write it in the notebook.

By thinking these thoughts of appreciation and realigning your energy with appreciation, which is truly of the love vibration, you are beginning the first step in transmuting the paradox. You are bringing the positive charge to the negative charge. You are using the inherent power found in working with the polarities of this experience. You are appreciating (positive, uplifting charge) and you are releasing yourself from Howard's wrath (the negative, draining charge.) This is how it starts and once you find the energy shifting with Howard and you will, continue to monitor your reactions to him. You want to continue working with the Aspects of Appreciation technique until you have created a neutral environment with Howard. And yes, you need to write these down. There is power when you write something down and move it out of you onto paper or an electronic device. It's cathartic on one hand and on the other hand, it's a bold statement to the universal energy. Once the situation feels more neutral than charged, you can honestly look at the external behavior of Howard as a reflection of your own internal world.

The Power of Choice

Always remember that the way in which you practice your free will, thus your freedom, is through the direction of your choice. You are constantly making choices in every moment. How you transform your circumstance is through your choice and not through the choices of others'. However, it may seem easier and appear to be a way out of a circumstance when you blame outside forces, including other people. Every time you point the finger at outside influences, you do not grow. You merely perpetuate the presenting circumstance.

You can choose to use the power of your choice as the energy needed to transform any given moment of conflict since choice is an element of transmutation. However, it must be made and directed with intentions that support your growth and not stagnation. You choose growth when you align yourself with the principle of neutrality for the highest good of all parties involved.

Here is an example that illustrates how this works. Let's say that you are extremely angry with someone you know. The anger is very intense and is tearing you apart emotionally. Physically, you are elevating your stress levels. Your adrenaline, cortisol and norepinephrine hormones are in attack and self-afflict mode. Being angry certainly isn't helping you on any level and in fact, it's depleting your energy force and causing havoc in your body. At this point you can choose to continue down this destructive path or you can choose to go down a constructive path.

This is a conscious choice you must make, as hard as it may be in the moment. If you choose the positive creative path, you may need to step away from the heated situation first, then proceed with the steps I'm about to explain. When you can calm down, ask yourself what just happened. Maintain an open heart to what had just transpired and be willing to observe your contribution to this event. Turn within yourself and choose what side of the event's polarity you wish to align. Again, you can choose to align with the destructive path or you can align with the constructive path. The constructive path means that you can transmute this heated energy into another form. Remember, you are the Alchemist of your life and in a moment you can transmute your thoughts and feelings, thus your reality.

Let's say you choose to go down the path of construction and not destruction this time. Then, let's explore the steps to constructively create and transform your reality:

1.) You choose to remove yourself from the heat of the moment, either mentally or physically. This choice alone provides you another option—an entirely new perspective—from becoming reactive.

2.) Next, you choose to transmute your anger through maintaining an open heart, while looking within and again choosing to constructively channel this energy in a new direction. Anger holds much potential energy. So, use this source of energy to propel yourself in the direction of creating growth.

3.) Now, look at the situation as mirroring your own internal struggles. In other words, ask yourself where inside of you do you feel a duplicate of what just transpired outwardly? Keep that heart open to hearing truth because in that moment you have chosen a path of construction, not destruction.

4.) Find that part in you that is fighting. Choose to shed light on it. This could take some time to discover. Looking within and reconciling this internal battle is part of your spiritual and personal work you need to do along this path.

This behavior does not mean you are backing out or avoiding the other person or circumstance. No, quite contrary! Instead, you have your own little secret and it is a secret internal acknowledgment that you choose where, how and with whom you will expend your energy. Instead of reacting in ways that are damaging to you and further damaging to the other party, you are claiming your empowerment. You are helping not only yourself, as you transmute this energy, you are assisting the overall energy surrounding the event to transmute. Now, this is real magic!

When you start to practice this, it will become more natural. You will learn that you can choose to capitalize upon all of your interactions, circumstances and events as a form of personal growth. Every single experience—yes, I mean **EVERY** single experience— you encounter along life's path is to shake and wake you up to your Divine Self. Understand that the Outerworld and the Innerworld are really one. They are the tail and the head of the same coin. For it is through your interactions with others in the Outerworld, as your mirror, where you get to view your progress with your Innerworld.

CHAPTER X
THE SACRED MARRIAGE

The Hieros Gamos is the sexual union of a sacred couple that takes place in the Innerworld or the Outerworld. The sacred couple can be the pairing of gods and goddesses or the union between a human and a god. In alchemical processes, it begins with the internal union of opposite energies—King and Queen—becoming the union of spirit with soul within the body. This Sacred Marriage recreates the Axis Mundi, Jacob's Ladder, The Above with the Below and The Sacred Tree of Life, to name a few. Around the globe and within many teachings of various mystery traditions, religions and theosophies, this union was honored in their sacred texts—the coming together of the energetic opposites found within the Sacred Masculine and Feminine Principles. They knew that once they reconciled the conflicting dualistic nature within themselves by clearing away the blocks to it, they transcended duality through the Sacred Marriage of the King and the Queen within. They understood that there is intrinsic value in each primordial principle and only by existing together in union, could the golden path leading to their internal and eternal salvation be found. By embracing each other in balance, something new emerges—the two will become the one. This One Thing is called the Philosopher's Stone and was that for which the Alchemists searched. It is best described as an intellect of feeling that can be elevated and purified, producing a perfect intuition and becoming the permanent golden state of consciousness. The message of the divine lovers reminds us that our love relationships can be gateways into expanded consciousness. In

Alchemical terms, the Philosopher's Stone is a direct gnosis of reality. The Emerald Tablet reminds the seeker of this state of awareness that, "all obscurity will be clear to you."

When the King and Queen unite, they combine the power of thoughts with the power of emotions and feelings. Therefore, The One Mind of the highest spirit is united with The One Thing of the greater soul. In alchemical traditions, the spirit is equated to the masculine aspect, whereas the soul is equated to the feminine aspect. When they come together within the Center of our Being in a dynamic interplay with each other, we find the eternal divine light. The Alchemists called this inner light, the Secret Fire of the inspired imagination, and used it to connect with the source of higher inspiration to quicken and transform their beings.

Within the Gnostic writings, which greatly influenced the Alchemists, they speak of the Divine Feminine Principle as a consort to the Divine Masculine Principle. In one of the Gnostics texts called The Sophia of Jesus Christ, Sophia, meaning "wisdom," represents the feminine aspect and consort of Jesus Christ. It reads:

> The Perfect Savior said, Son of Man harmonized
> with Sophia, his consort, and revealed a great
> androgynous light. His male name is called Savior,
> Begetter of All Things. His female name is called
> All Begettress Sophia.

In the Western tradition, the archetype of the divine lovers survived mostly within secretly hidden texts, alchemical formulas, mystery religions and iconic artwork. Within the early Christian church, the image of the Virgin Mary retained many aspects of being the divine consort, an advocate and the queen. In many of the religious artwork from the Middle Ages, the Virgin Mary fulfills this divine role as she is depicted siting with Christ as his queen and equal, as "the queen who is by the right side of the king."

However, I know I'm not alone when I ask this question, "Where is Jesus' consort, beyond the art images that show his mother fulfilling this role?" Nowhere in the Bible does it state that Jesus was celibate or not married. In the original Jewish tradition, for Jesus to be recognized as a spiritual teacher, it was more common than not for such a teacher to be married. This is one mystery we may never know the answer, however, there are texts that allude to it.

In the non-canonical gospels there is reference to the nature of Mary Magdalene's relationship with Jesus. In one passage in The Gospel of Philip it reads, "There were three who always walked with the Lord: Mary his mother and her sister and Magdalene, the one who was called his companion." In another passage within the same Gospel it reads:

> And the companion of the Savior is Mary Magdalene. But Christ loved her more than all the disciples and used to kiss her often on her mouth. The rest of the disciples were offended by it and expressed disapproval. They said to him, 'Why do you love her more than all of us?' The Savior answered and said to them, 'Why do I not love you like her?' When a blind man and one who sees are both together in darkness, they are no different from one another. Then the light comes, then he who sees will see the light, and he who is blind will remain in darkness.

Union by Dream

Many years ago, Dr. Coletta Long, a mentor, friend and colleague of mine shared the following dream with me that splendidly exemplifies a version of the sacred union of the King and Queen. The dream had just occurred a few nights prior and Coletta was still feeling very moved by the experience. The dream never left me either as it felt archetypal, leaving an impression on me as well. I could see that my friend was emotionally touched in an empowered way because of it.

Within the dream, Coletta wakens to beings entering her room and telling her that she must go with them quickly, as her arrival is being waited upon. Without hesitation, she leaves with the beings and she travels with them through a brilliant light taking them into a beautifully decorated reception hall within a palatial building. Coletta describes seeing gorgeous flowers decorating the hall along with abundant food laid out along banquet tables. She sees the finest linens, golden plates, stemware and flatware on the tables, flanked by large pillars. Everything is in white and gold. People, dressed in their finest garbs, are arriving and they all seem to know my friend. Coletta remembers feeling comfortable within their presence. She looks down and sees that she is now wearing a flowing white gown and not the attire she was wearing when she went to bed. Coletta asks one of the beings who has escorted her to this mystical place, "What are they all doing here?" This being looks straight upon her and says, "They are all here for your wedding." In that moment, she is ushered up the hall in between the rich banquet tables to the front. As my friend described to me, standing there and awaiting her is a handsome young man wearing a white uniform. He says to her, "I have been waiting for you, my love." Coletta told me that she felt such a sense of belonging, a knowing and a deep love from this man and all in attendance. She accepts the sacrament of marriage and then she wakes up back in her bed. It felt all too real to her, as the dream was lucid and brilliant. Back in her bed she wanted nothing more than to return to that place, but she was thankful for that deeply gratifying archetypal experience. She felt changed. When I asked Coletta what her thoughts were about the dream, she declared whole-heartedly without a doubt she had experienced the sacred marriage of her Divine Feminine to her Divine Masculine.

Union by Oracle

It is so fitting and actually synchronistic that two of the main guides with whom I communicate via the Great Oracle are The SUN and The MOON—the influence of the masculine principle and the feminine principle respectively! I met them two decades ago and their teachings have always been insightful and profound, but our work together took an interesting turn a few years ago. It all started before the time of the Venus' Gathering of Goddesses; the Oracle started referring to me as CEO and not as Karen. Well, I found that amusing; it was a fitting pet name, but at the time I didn't understand the implications of this shift in naming conventions. Although, when I inquired why, they replied, "Well, you are a CEO of a company after all."

Yes, that is true. I am the Chief Executive Officer and have been for many years of the utility design and consulting company I started in the telecommunication's industry. Although the title is reserved for corporate documents and signing contracts with clients, I always refer to myself as a Director of Operations. For years, many of the players in my industry didn't even know I owned the company. I actually like it that way.

What was to happen next, I was not expecting; yet, I was on the verge of gaining a new perspective. A friend and I sat down for a session with the Great Oracle on the Fourth of July, 2012. The SUN and The MOON began the communications by telling me it was time to drop the CEO title. They told me they would now refer to me as the Queen. They explained that for a while, I was aligning more with the masculine side of my energies rather than more fully including his complement, the feminine polarity. They felt a shift within me that started over the past couple of years and was now culminating as inner flexibility to this dynamic balance. I was spiraling back and returning full circle, allowing the feminine side of my energies to reemerge and complement the masculine energies through balance.

Well, they were right. Until a couple years prior to that point, the qualities I favored in my internal processes for operating my business, aligned with the energetic traits of the masculine polarity. Looking back on it, this alignment made sense when coming from a purely physical approach. Many of the people who performed my end of site development for new "cell towers" were construction managers, general contractors, public utilities and mostly men. Man, could I could run with the best of them while being aligned with the masculine side of my nature, represented by the traditional archetype of the CEO. However, in my work, I was neglecting the feminine side of my nature, as she was mostly shoved to the side during the business week, which became business evenings, turning into business weekends. The over-powering masculine side of me was driving me to exhaustion, working up to sixteen to eighteen hours a day for extended periods of time. It was so bad that I became internally sick, creating stress that caused havoc on my thyroid. In 2011, I reclaimed my life and started back on the path to reclaiming my Divine Feminine.

The SUN and The MOON wanted to make it clear to me that it never mattered what type of work I did, whether I was running my company, writing a book or teaching dance; they definitely wanted me to understand that the masculine and feminine polarities were both crucial to each other. The fullness of their expression and my expression could only occur when they were together, complementing each other's energies. To further emphasize this point, they said to me, "All work is a benefit as long as you are vibrating at the right freQUEENcy." (They included the QUEEN within frequency as a reflection of my inner work—clever!) It is not considered a benefit when the work or task at hand lowers one's frequency. When a pastime is truly enjoyed, the vibration is energized and will elevate one's frequency. They say that makes all the difference for experiencing joy in the moment or not.

So, from the Fourth of July and onward, they renamed me the Queen because I was honoring my Divine Feminine and bringing her back to the King. The Queen is empowered from this space of feminine energy, when her King has her back. Divine Feminine internal qualities such as, receptivity, acceptance, intuition and trust were included within my experiences as opposed to predominately embracing the external masculine CEO qualities of dominance, assertion and control. Eureka! I struck the golden shades of gray found between these polar opposites. Quite literally speaking, this was my Declaration of Independence Day. This was the day I felt it and was acknowledged by the Spirit Friends for coming full circle and bringing the Queen to the King so they could exist together in a sweet embrace. Not only were fire works exploding in the distant, sparks were igniting within me. Quite honestly, my King was getting lonely, but he would never admit that when he's fighting a battle! Instead we must admit it ourselves.

The inner work of bringing these two together brought me to another level of co-creation, connection and gnosis. As a matter of fact, I was so influenced by this inner union and that session, it became my inspiration for writing this book! The Hips to Heart breathing exercise came out of my quest to maintain an inner balance between my internal King and Queen energies. I started sharing the power of the Queen with my women friends, teaching them to allow her energies to become more fully engaged within their lives. The vibes had changed and people were noticing and commenting, as we moved through life with quiet confidence from our little secret.

As we welcome the Queen and all she represents, not only do we come to know our greater Self, we come to know the greater cosmos. Source wants us to express both energies together, as they provide clarity for how the universe can support us. Knowing more about ourselves found in the transmutation of duality, we are able to consciously co-create our desires, not create by default, but create by awareness. The Queen is supported, honored and cherished by her King and I felt this within, once I allowed them to co-exist in union. Although I still experience the opposite energies co-existing within their dynamic interplay, I am keenly aware of the process, as my personal work continues within the alchemical crucible of transformation.

The sacred marriage of these polarities within is truly the underlying sacred principle of the universe. It is the cosmic blueprint! The union of these opposites create a balance and harmony necessary to easily move between the two realms of matter and spirit—the Below and the Above. This internal union is divine as it restores the partnership paradigm that our ancestors of the ancient civilizations knew. Reverence for this fundamental union helps heals the human psyche, by reminding us of our inner authority and bringing us to an alignment with the seat of our soul, our heart, our Center, within a new fullness of experience. Now, we can reach into the Light of the Whole Universe.

CHAPTER XI
SOURCE

The Higher Self

When you feel the most "Present" within yourself with a capital "P," you are aligned with your Higher Self. You are present within yourself, experiencing "you" beyond the limitations of the ego personality, extending into a knowing of "you" as a spiritual being. This is the "you" that existed before you were born into your current physical body and it is the "you" that exists forever in eternity. The Higher Self is your Divine Spark that connects you back to your Creator—back to the Source.

My Spirit Friends tell me that we align with our Higher Selves when we "plug in." We plug in by getting out of the way of our rational and judgmental minds and make an internal shift within our awareness that promotes transmission. We must use a process of fine-tuning our awareness from our rambling, internal chatter to one of focused intention for reception. It is an act of shifting our thoughts and feelings from running amuck to reining them in by intending "how" we will use our thoughts and feelings. This process requires a clarity in awareness. In fact, my Spirit Friends say that we make our way through life by seeking a "path of clarity."

Constantly, we are making choices within our lives and this occurs in every moment of the day. Choices can seem as small as the thoughts we choose to think in the moment, the roadways we choose to travel as we drive to and from work, the foods we choose to purchase at the grocery store to eat and the people we choose to include within the circle we call our friends. How we exist within life stems from the choices we make. Often we make choices that leave us in pain or in misery. We also make choices that inspire, challenge us or bring us much happiness. Whether we are conscious or unconscious of the myriad choices we make at any given moment, we are making choices and energy is aligning around those choices. We gain clarity as we learn to make each new choices for our lives from a place of greater awareness and consciousness. Greater awareness grows as we deepen ourselves into the observations of our Innerworlds. The more we explore our Innerworlds, we will discover the strengths they hold, but only after we confront the illusions we currently clutch. As we dig deep within, we will find the hidden treasure in time, which is the golden light of our Higher Selves.

Now having said this, doesn't mean that you will always choose the smoothest path to life, as the smoothest path is not always the answer to the Higher Self. The Higher Self, your Divine Spark, always drives you towards evolution and growth. Those times in life when you cry out, "why me?" are the precise events and circumstances you needed in order to move up to the next level of awareness and consciousness. Your Higher Self loves you; it will never place you in harms way. It honors the totality of itself, including the aspect that is you, incarnated in your physical form. It would never lead you astray or down what you may consider the "wrong path."

During a conversation with my Higher Self via the Great Oracle, my Higher Self asked me, "Do you believe in your Higher Self?" I answered yes. Then my Higher Self said:

> You are always on the path to a higher vibration. You must trust. Just believe that you would never make a decision that was not good for you. This message is universal. Few are willing to seek it [path of higher vibration]. You will never be perfect but you continue to seek. That is the answer.

Your Higher Self always has your best intentions as it guides you on your path, encouraging you to awaken to your true north.

Your ego personality has its hang-ups and will create the obstacles and barriers you find yourself up against. These hang-ups are kept hidden in the recesses of your mind. You discover what they are when you find yourself repeating some of the same trials and tribulations again and again. These experiences serve as guideposts, showing you what is hidden and what needs to be uncovered. The hang-ups stem from your limiting beliefs about life and about yourself. You may have learned these beliefs in school, at home or from any number of social groups or institutions. For the most part, you come to maintain what you've learned or what's been explained to you from the multitude of environments you traverse. These beliefs exist, just like your choices, whether or not you explore the validity of them. Your Higher Self would consider many of these beliefs "false beliefs" that become obstacles to plugging in. They are false because you consume and regurgitate them without much awareness and without much clarity.

The entire goal of the Alchemists was to be in communion and connection with that Divine Higher Self—thus, the Source. They transmuted the obstacles that kept them from knowing the divinity within themselves. They brought the conflicting aspects of themselves to the forefront and transformed those thoughts and emotions—those false beliefs—that created the tension and conflict. Observation, exploration, practice and meditation provided internal harmony so they could listen and hear their Higher Selves. They strived to develop this union internally first, then with the Source. Experiencing this union is the same as experiencing your Center. It is the Higher Self and it is Source. It is within this space of unification, where balance is found. It is precisely that space where you find inner peace and contentment within your life, along your path and its unfolding journey, no matter where it leads you or where you direct it. Being in this space is where your true empowerment resides.

Through the Great Oracle, a new Being of Light entered my life in 1992, providing many healing messages over the years. I always referred to him as being male in gender, although, the light beings are genderless. They will appear to take on characteristics of either the masculine principle or the feminine principle energies, depending upon your comfort. This Being's name is HEALING SPIRIT and he often comes forward when someone at a session requires emotional healing or spiritual fine-tuning. He is extremely helpful and supportive, yet direct in his words. After being in communication with him for nineteen years, The MOON told me, "HEALING SPIRIT loves you very much." She further told me that "he is always watching out" for me. "Know that H.S. is HEALING SPIRIT and H.S. is Higher Self. He is one in the same." What? I asked for clarification. Did The MOON just say that HEALING SPIRIT is in fact my Higher Self? She told me that is precisely so, thus the reason why he had a name with the same initials.

I thoroughly enjoyed speaking with HEALING SPIRIT when he came through the Great Oracle, as I still do to this day. I most certainly felt a familiarity and comfort about him. I found it extremely interesting, the stealthy manner in which my Higher Self disguised itself as HEALING SPIRIT. At that time I thought how this really speaks to the possibility that all of us are already in touch with our Higher Selves and have that direct line of communication. Further conversations with the Spirit Friends, revealed that it is true that we are always connected to our Higher Selves. They say we can't be removed from our Higher Selves. However, we can remain **unplugged**. We may not understand the difference and we may not know how to recognize the Higher Self's voice from the inner voice of the ego or personality. They coexist, but the ego can often drown it out. Yet, with practice, everyone can learn to plug in and hear the guiding presence of the Higher Self.

The Higher Self's presence within your life is one of patience and gentle guidance. It knows you from a larger perspective, so it clearly understands the path you create for yourself and its resulting trajectory. It intervenes within your life through synchronistic events. To consciously know the presence of your Higher Self, requires the contact initiated from your end. It will never leave you; it can't! It is you and then so much more of you that exists beyond your personality and your physical body, spanning your awareness and beyond comprehension. It knows "big people in big places," as it is an aspect of the greatest Source of all, God. To know this Source is to learn how to get your personality, the ego Self, out of the way and learn to not only listen to the voice of your Higher Self, but to really hear it.

Plugging In

The Higher Self is always with us and ever-present. However, for the most part, many people are not even cognizant of this concept of Self or even mindful that they can attain this level of spiritual expansion. They certainly weren't taught this in school and it's not a typical topic of conversation while sitting around the kitchen table. Others may have heard about the Higher Self concept, but without much comprehension or understanding of it. It's often seen as something that is "out there," unattainable to personal knowing. Others, who do know about it, may not know that they can strengthen the communion, thus increase the communication between the personal Self and the Higher Self. They may not realize that they have a plug and all they have to do is find the Higher Self's socket and plug into it. It really can be that easy to do, once they do the work that clears away the blockages to the socket.

You know when you are plugged into your Higher Self because you have a sense of clarity about your life. You see how things are stacking up and where you are headed by the choices you make. You find that you think clearly, thus making decisions and choices with great ease, often not second-guessing yourself. You have heard people say, "trust your gut" or "trust your intuition." Well, this is similar to "going with your knowing" when you are plugged into your Higher Self. When you are plugged in, you gain a more objective view towards life than when you are unplugged. When there are struggles with others, instead of pushing to be right, you endeavor to find the best solution for all parties involved. Being plugged in encourages your desire to see the opposing viewpoints at the same time and work to find a common ground solution. You are willing to make changes, as change become the spice to your life.

When you are plugged into your Higher Self, it's as if you have received an additional boost of energy to your system. You may feel a sense of growing excitement in the moment, drawing blissful experiences that leave you feeling an incredible sense of awe to the beauty surrounding you. Life can feel that much sweeter, as you thrive to take notice of your beautiful surroundings, sunsets, sunrises and all of life in between. You notice the beauty in the smallest of things, such as that flower that has endeavored to grow through a crack in the sidewalk. You feel your connection to others and a deepening of empathy towards them. You may feel an overwhelming sense of peace or love unexpectedly.

Being plugged in is when you are at your best and you feel on top of the world, as if nothing can go wrong. You feel "on" as if all is aligned in your universe and an epiphany is coming. It's as if all of a sudden, the world makes sense and you are right where you need to be right now. Well, in fact, you are! At some time or another, every single one of us has had such moments. Being in communion with your Higher Self promotes these types of interconnected, synchronistic moments. The goal is to spend more and more of your waking time plugged in. When you are asleep, you are already plugged in. It's when you are awake that you will have the most struggles staying plugged in. Yet with practice, you can learn to spend more and more time plugged into your Higher Self, your Center. Plugging in gifts you with a conscious awareness of your Center that connects you back to Source—hearing and feeling God.

When you are not plugged in, it becomes much easier to feel disconnected within your life. You may not trust others because often you don't trust yourself. You may have a tendency to second-guess your decisions and replay them countless times within your head, even if this decision occurred many, many years earlier. When you are unplugged, you may not make the best decisions either. You know this from your past experiences. When you are learning to plug in, you will find yourself vacillating between feeling connected to life and then feeling disconnected.

As a more comprehensive understanding of plugging into your Higher Self is developing, you may still fall back frequently to what my Spirit Friends call your "comfort food." When you are learning something new, it's very easy to regress. Stretching yourself to grow can be extremely trying, as it will test you to push beyond your comfort zones. As you expand the walls of your world and what you thought you knew, it feels as if you are learning a new way to walk. During these times, you will need to practice patience and gentility with yourself. It will take time for getting used to inhabiting your newly expanded consciousness. The Spirit Friends want to make sure you know that as a human, you cannot be plugged in to your Higher Self all of the time. Your human nature is just as important as your spiritual nature. They ask that you do not punish yourself when you are not. See this as a process that you are developing, but also know that even when you unplug, you are still moving forwards in evolution. They say that although you fall back, you cannot fail. As with anything, practice makes perfect. As you continue down this path with practice, you will recognize when you swing out of this awareness and remember how to return to your Center more readily and easily.

Practice being plugged into your Higher Self whenever you can, especially when you are not distracted and within the comfort and solace of your own home. You can practice all of the available plugging in techniques and determine which ones work the best for you. This way, when you find yourself within a tough and sticky situation, such as a disagreement with another, you can pull out your toolbox of techniques and try one after another until you find the one that works for you in that given moment. Each situation may require a different tool. Each moment is different from the last as you are also different in the next moment. Your practice and tools will change as you change and evolve in each new moment. This is a lesson in progression.

The resulting benefits of being plugged into your Higher Self, as much as possible, are far-reaching. You will learn to make better decisions for yourself from within this newfound awareness. This awareness helps you relate to other people in your environments and circumstances in which you spend your time. Being plugged in lets you notice the aliveness of the world, filling you moment by moment with inspiration. In this space you access the divine inherent spark of creativity, enabling the expansion of your creative thoughts into your world. You are connected, you feel centered and you acknowledge your ability to orchestrate beautiful moments reflected from your Source to continue to create the life of your desires.

Techniques to Plug In

Your Higher Self, and for that matter, any of your guides, have a difficult time communicating clearly when you are unplugged. Let us explore ways that can assist you to know your Center, thus plug into your Higher Self. All of these tools help support the region of your heart, as you practice reclaiming the domain of the mysterious feminine principle and her reign over the realm of the imaginal.

Expanding Light

This tool is one of the most essential tools you will learn to access and use. It quickly became my most important tool and a staple within all of my spiritual work. Once I directly experienced the power of this tool, whether used for myself or with others, I elevated it to a cornerstone position within many areas of my life. This tool is the eternal flame within you—your own internal light. The Alchemists called it the Secret Fire of the inspired imagination. This metaphorical flame is your connection and reminder of the spark of Source from the Creator God that resides within every living, sentient being. Literally, it is the place within in you that resonates with your connection back to Source. You feel it. You know it. You access it through the imaginal realm of your being.

First, you will need to recognize it with your mind. Others may feel it within their bodies at first, but either way, I'm suggesting you get in touch with it and learn its use. Begin this process by sitting still within a space where you are uninterrupted and have the freedom to focus. Now, imagine within you a spark of light. This spark of light will appear in the part of your body that feels right for you. As you witness this spark, just take it in. See it, feel it and allow it to expand. Watch and feel as it expands within your body. Use the power of your imagination to help it expand. This is an eternal flame that is always burning. It has always been in you and it will always be with you. No matter how hard it may be to find it, feel it or sense it at times, it's there. Sometimes you cloud it over, cover it up, hide it or avoid it. Nevertheless, even if you can't find it right now, it is there. With your mind's eye let it expand further, filling your body with light. Once your body is full of this expanded eternal flame, allow it to penetrate your skin and expand further out. This light is from an infinite Source so it radiates permanently. This light is your connection back to Source and it is your connection to your Higher Self. Your Higher Self resides in your physical body, but expands out into infinity. As you expand your light further and further out and beyond, your awareness expands with the light. Your awareness, fueled by this light, connects with your Higher Self. Now, you exist as a being of light, reminding yourself of your origins. This light is a powerful light since it is your hologram of the Source. This light can be used as a tool for clarity, wisdom, guidance and healing when you focus its beam with the power of your intentions. You choose how and where you want to use it. Revel in feeling full of light, expanding until it exists not only within, but also into your aura and beyond. Stay in this space as long as you wish, but before you return from this visualization, tell yourself that you allow your body to remain within the experience and presence of its light.

Understand that this light can do powerful feats when you work with it over time and learn how to engage and maintain it. It is the "white light" people speak about when they ask for protection. Not only is this white light from our guides, angels, protectors and Source, but it is also from and of you. Remember to merge your powerful internal light with the light of your guides. Your guides want you to know how to use your own light, in addition to calling upon divine light, thus divine help. The more you work with your light within, the more you will be able to use this light to transmute negative experiences and fears, as well as strengthen yourself within your spiritual growth and pursuits.

Light Work

Light work has far-reaching and timeless applications not contained by the space and time continuum. It can be a powerful agent for alchemical transmutation, transforming the past, present and future. Following, are some examples of its use.

Past Lives

When I was working as a therapist in private practice, I would use hypnosis and regression therapy as a tool for exploring deep-rooted causes to a presenting condition—the reason why the client entered therapy. Employing hypnotic techniques, I would regress the client back to a time when the presenting condition started—back to its source. The client regressed to where she needed to go by trusting her intuition as I guided her into deeper levels of consciousness. Most often, the client would find herself popping into a previous life since the root of the presenting issue took her there. Once within this previous life recall, we would explore the life to arrive at the cause of the issue. While exploring the life or multiple lives, we would come face to face with extremely painful events. We would address the atrocities and resulting pain by using the powerful light within to transmute, thus transform, the scene in which she was attached and now reliving. Each regressed client was taught to access and use the internal light and shine it upon that life's pain to dislodge it from the client's "soul-ular" memory. Nothing was ever extracted and removed. Instead, through the regression work, the client learned to integrate the life's lessons. Using the internal light became the client's mode and means towards healing the pain from the past (or concurrent) life.

In-Between Lives

After working through the pain from the recalled life during the session, the client was guided into her death scene where she transitioned from that life into the "in-between" life. If the client still felt any residue of pain during the transition, we would employ the eternal light to assist with relieving the residual pain from the prior life until she could transition peacefully. After this transition was made and explored, we would move to her "life review." In this in-between place, the soul reviews its life that was just released with the help of other light beings. In this period of honest review, the truth is revealed as to what lessons she learned and what lessons she missed. However, sometimes there may be a period of time in the afterlife, where the transitioned soul may have felt lost, earthbound, frightened and unable to go into the light of Source upon death. Under these circumstances, the client and I would work with her eternal light within, using it as a beacon, escorting the client through her fears by removing the barriers and working her way back into the light of the afterworld. Truly the past can be changed! By time traveling, via the vehicle of consciousness, one can return to previous incarnations and release stored up pain the soul is holding, thus change the conditions that have carried over and are appearing in life now.

Current Lives

When I work with the Great Oracle, communicating with the deceased, my guides, angels and other realms of consciousness, I always invoke my sacred light within. I begin the session with the "hips to heart" breathing, allowing the breath to expand and spread my light throughout my entire body, while permeating beyond it. The light fills me up and spills out. Then, I state an invocation, calling upon the Divine White Light of Source to surround us, protect us and share with us. The key is that not only do I receive protection from without, I have my protection from within already established. The Above and the Below unite.

There is an inherent healing quality within this light source. This light source can be directed with your mind's eye and feeling center throughout your body as a pathway, sending health. Try focusing on the light and sending it's transformative qualities to the next headache you have. Visualize and feel the light envelop the pain and dissolve it, releasing it from your body with your breath. You can use this light source to ease tension in your body. Send it where you need it to go and allow the light to cloak the tension within a blanket of peace and relaxation. The ways in which you can work with your light is infinite! Just remember, the more you use it, the stronger it will become and the more readily you'll be able to tap into it.

The Healing Sun

During a recent session with the Great Oracle, one of the participants, Joe, who was also acting as the session scribe began shaking and moving his arm around. I didn't think much about it until I felt a shock—like an electric shock—hitting my elbow at the same moment this participant was shaking his arm. I screeched out, "ow!" I removed my hands from the planchette and asked Joe what he was doing, as I had just received a shock from what seemed to be coming from his shaking arm and flicking fingers. I was located a mere thirty inches away from Joe's arm when he was doing this. Joe had a huge smile on his face and said that he couldn't believe what had just happened. He felt shocks to his right arm, the arm that had severe pain in it for years without relief and was now moving his arm around painlessly in amazement. It sure seemed that Joe had flung some of those shocks at me while he was shaking his arm. The moment before this happened, we were communicating with The SUN (one of my guides); so we asked The SUN what had just happened. The SUN told us that his energy sent electrical energy to Joe's arm. After further clarification with The SUN, we learned that Joe received far-infrared energy from The SUN (and sun) in the form of an electrical charge that removed the pain in his arm. During another session, two months later with Joe present, we requested The SUN to speak further about Joe's arm, which continued to be pain-free. The SUN told us that "we choose our pain and we choose our health" and at that time, Joe was ready to choose healing in his arm; so all they did was help remove the obstacle. To this day, Joe's right arm remains pain-free.

Meditation

Still body meditation is the typical way many have come to think of meditation, although there are meditation practices that include movement of the body or a deliberate state of mindfulness during activities. No matter which form of meditation you choose to practice, all share the fundamental principle to quiet your busy mind through inner contemplation and reflection.

Still Body

There are many formal methods for this type of meditation, stemming from spiritual traditions. Here I am simply sharing a blend comprised of various forms of meditations that I have tried over the years. The practice I have in place now is working very well for me, although, I do find that it changes and evolves as I change. However, I suggest you explore some of the different types and find one or a blend of a few that resonates for you.

Begin still meditation with sessions of at least fifteen minutes in duration, eventually progressing up to thirty minutes at a time. Find a time that will work within your schedule when you can meditate daily during a consistent time frame. After sitting in your private, undistracted space, close your eyes and allow your breath to take you inside. Follow the rhythm of your breath, noticing how it begins to slow down. Next, allow your mind to enter into the breath, slowing down as well. Now, close your mind to thoughts and images. This is quite a bit harder than it sounds because once you stop and close your eyes you will begin to notice how much rift-raft of information is swirling around in your mind at any given moment. It will seem like chaos is in there, as you try to silence the inner chatter, noise and confusion. You can try to let it float on by without holding onto the thoughts. You will probably fight yourself with this. Strange feelings, thoughts and body sensations can bubble up to the surface. As you sit and allow the thoughts to move on by, try to not become attached to them. In the beginning and for some time, you will find your mind staying with some of the swirling thoughts, taking you on tangents to process and think about them—more inner chatter! This happens. This is the process. Be patient with yourself and keep on trying, each and every day you meditate. As your focus wanders, gently bring your focus back to no thoughts and away from the thoughts. Continue to do this during each session. It will feel like a constant game of yo-yo, reining your thoughts back to your silent mind without thoughts, only to take you away again. This is the ebb and flow of the process for learning meditation. Every time, just gently bring your mind back to a state of nothingness.

Silently repeating a sacred word or mantra as you sit in meditation, such as, love, peace and "om" can help you keep that focus by focusing on one word and one thought. Personally, I work with a feeling. The feeling I choose is love and as I sit in meditation, I allow myself to recall what love feels like and expand that feeling within my body from my hips to my heart, expanding it throughout my body. Then I allow that feeling to expand beyond my body and into the cosmos. Once this feeling encompasses my awareness, I work to float in these feelings without thinking about them.

Still body meditation is worth doing because within a short amount of time (varies from individual to individual), you will begin to feel the benefits of spending time in meditation. For your health and well-being, it delivers a sense of relaxation, stress reduction and mental confidence, as you free yourself from the binds of your incessant, inner banter. It can also aid in depression, help lower blood pressure and relieve anxiety and insomnia, to name a few other health benefits. My favorite benefit from meditation is how it draws me closer to experiencing the interconnected, primordial energy of the universe. I often receive guidance and insights from my

Higher Self and Spirit Friends, as an after effect to my meditations. I enter a state of enlivened receptivity.

Active Body

I tried still body meditation many years ago, discovering that I just couldn't get into it back then like I can now. I was okay with that because I found myself engaging in other practices that still allowed me to quiet my mind and experience that connection I love. Yoga and spiritual movement, such as tribal belly dancing, took me into meditative-like states. The breath work, the repetitive movements and the sacred postures allowed me to work with the fundamental principles found in meditation. I found my Center and peace of mind when pursuing such active meditations through the vehicle of my body.

Although mindful meditation can be practiced while sitting still, it can also be practiced in an active state. This type of meditation invites you to give deliberate thought and concentration, while being mindful and aware of everything you do in your life. You are focused in the moment and being of the moment, yet not trying to be any different than how you currently are. These principles help you become unconditionally present with whatever is happening, no matter what it is. In this practice, you place a nonjudgmental attention on the details of your experience as they arise and subside, without rejecting anything. Being mindful allows you to show up for your life instead of wishing for things to be different or becoming distracted by your experiences.

Walking meditation is another active body practice that involves mindfulness. Basically, in the practice, you walk with awareness and presence to the experience. The walk is not about getting somewhere; instead it is a stroll where you bask in the journey of the walk and the beauty all around. Each step is made with the intention of peace, while the ground supports each step. You relax your body and arms, slowly taking one step at a time with a smile on your face.

Journaling

Have you ever kept a diary, opening it periodically to pen your intimate secrets and commentary on life? I received my first diary when I was eight years old. (It was the year of my first Ouija Board and my first journal—hmmmm—what a prophetic combination, given I would keep copious journals from my spirit communications!) Now, this diary was not an ordinary diary; it was a bright yellow Holly Hobbie themed diary that was soft and squishy to the touch. Do you remember that character? Well, I still have it and keep it in the company of the other journals I've kept over the years. I loved that diary because it came with a lock and key and that meant all of my secrets and thoughts were kept safe with that little golden key. Unbeknownst to me, anyone could pick the lock with a safety pin, which I found out after one of my brothers found my diary and picked it. I felt devastated about that, but it didn't stop me from journaling. I just got wiser and stashed my diaries and journals in secret spaces, while living at home with curious brothers.

You too may have kept a diary when you were younger, but may have let the practice of writing in it fall to the wayside as you became an adult. Other pursuits took its place and you can't find the value in writing down your thoughts anyway. Maybe you don't know where to start or how to journal? That is a common response I hear from people when I bring up the practice of journaling. So, let's address the reasons for journaling and how one goes about it?

Quite simply, journaling is a direct path to personal growth. I highly recommend it. For me, keeping a journal all these years has enriched my life in most profound ways. It creates intimacy with yourself, when you write about your life and the observations you are making. The more you write in your journal, the more observant you will become, for the observations provide openings into meaning and further explorations. Journaling becomes a way to notice your feelings. When you write your feelings about a specific situation that happened earlier in the day, you connect once again with those feelings in the moment. This helps you connect with your heart, your Center, and open to these feelings in another way. While writing, you can process them, you can release them and you can reflect upon them. Journaling becomes a channel to ask questions of yourself and through the writing, often times, you'll receive or find an answer. Writing takes you into the intuitive side of your brain where you can view issues and problems from a creative standpoint as opposed to the left-brain analytical view when you just talk about them.

1.) To begin, first decide if you are going to write in a paper journal or in an electronic format. I still choose to write freehand in a paper journal because not only do I like the tactile aspect of it, I also like the ease of being able to use it whenever and wherever, especially when a computer may not be accessible.

2.) Then, the next important aspect to journaling is to know that there are no rules! Maintain its privacy so you can write for yourself without censorship and not worry about an audience. Now, you have total freedom to write anything and everything you want.

3.) Begin anywhere. Don't worry about punctuation or correct grammar and spelling. Write quickly. If need be, pick a theme to start, such as a topic from this book. Explore your thoughts about it. Let it flow.

Dreams

When you are within the dream state, you cannot help but be plugged into your Higher Self! Your soul revels within this fluid realm of infinite possibilities, feeding your Higher Self with metaphorical images and symbols personally related to you. You are connected to the depth and breadth of yourself within your dreams.

Sleeping Dreams

Everyone dreams. You may not recall your dreams, but nevertheless, you have dreams. In fact, if you get six to eight hours of sleep each night, you will have on average four to six dreams during this time. Dreams occur during the rapid eye movement (REM) stages of your sleep. They will progressively increase in length as you sleep through the night, with your longest dream occurring right before you wake up. There is speculation to what purpose a dream serves and there are many thoughts to what those might be. Quite frankly, research and scientist just aren't sure. Nevertheless, dreams are very informative, interesting and often very insightful.

Everyone can learn dream recall. It is just a matter of programming yourself to remember your dreams. Place a pad of paper and writing utensil next to your bed where you can grab it and write as soon as you wake up with a dream. This pad of paper signals your subconscious mind that you are serious about your intent to recall your dreams. You can also use a recording device, as it signals your subconscious too. Before you go to sleep, make the request to yourself that you will remember your dreams and off to sleep you go.

Now, if you wake up in the middle of the night with a dream, don't kid yourself into believing you will remember it in the morning. Most likely you will not or you will loose a good portion of it. Instead, grab your pad and write down the dream right then. If you don't wake up until the morning, take the time to write what you recall of any dreams you had upon awakening. This could be a feeling state you had when you woke. It could be a few snippets of images you remember or words and people you recall. Just write them all down. Do this before you get out of the bed and begin your morning routine. Once you step foot out of the bed, the dream will begin to fade. Don't try to make any sense of the dreams, as dreams don't follow the typical linear progression that events in your walking life follow. They are all over the place. If you don't recall your dreams right away, have patience. They will reveal themselves to you with your dedication and persistence to this practice. As you record your dreams in your dream journal, you may notice themes emerging and a repertoire of symbols, places and people coming forth.

Lucid Dreams

Once you are able to recall your dreams, you may be able to have lucid dreams. Lucid dreaming means that you are consciously aware that you are dreaming while still in the dream state. In this type of awareness you can transform what is happening within the dream. For example, if there is something chasing you, you know that this is a dream, so you take a risk, turn around and ask the pursuer what he wants. Maybe you realize you are dreaming and choose to fly away.

Lucid dreaming is the opportunity to bring your conscious awareness to the dreamscape and co-create the dream reality. Reaching this level of dreaming, affords you the opportunities to travel all over the dreamscape and possibly meet your guides, visit far-away places or simply have a blast, flying around and exploring the environment.

When I was in graduate school, I joined a dream group sponsored by a member of the Association for Research and Enlightenment (A.R.E.), which is Edgar Cayce's foundation. We met weekly, exploring our dream symbolism, the inherent messages and lucid dreaming techniques. Before the last class, the group leader told us that we were to meet within a lucid group dream. We picked the night it was to happen and we picked the symbol we would see in the dream that would remind us to become lucid. The symbol we picked was a light bulb. Once we saw the light bulb in the dream, it was our sign to meet up with the rest of the group. What we didn't discuss was where this light bulb would be located. We returned to class the next week after having attempted the experiment. Several of us in the class reported finding the light bulb with a chain attached to it and pulling it. Once the light came on, we found ourselves staring at the other group members. I was one of the participants who was able to do this. There were two in the group who said they couldn't do it. Yet, the rest of us who were able to see each other within the group dream saw all of the group members. The strangest part of this experiment is that all of us, who turned the light on, saw that we were standing in a circle within a room of some sort. Our dreamscape images linked up.

Waking Dreams

This is a type of dream you have while you are actually awake. Purposefully, you use the faculties of your imagination and enter your own waking dream state. Also known as "active imagination," you can use this state of awareness to further explore experiences from your subconscious that have surfaced within you. Let's say you have a repeating image or theme from your dreams (written down in your dream journal, of course) that you want to understand further. You allow yourself to relax and go within by using one of the previously discussed techniques. Next, you focus on the image, allowing it to reveal more about itself to you. Without judgment, you observe the image and allow it to unfold. Most likely, other images will come or a story will begin to appear. Follow it. When you get to a place of curiosity about it, you can engage with it by asking questions. Through this process, the image from your dream is taking you on a guided meditation of its own and you are learning through observation first, then through interaction. The image is alive and it has a message or experience for you.

Art-making

"Oh no!" I can hear you shout from the pages, even as I write this. "I don't know how to draw!" Trust me, I hear that excuse often, in order to avoid this process. However, what I want to share with you is the value of using art in a free, expressive form for plugging into your Higher Self. This is not about creating beautiful artwork. Let's get beyond that and think of this as one more tool for you to have in your toolbox. Art can assist you by maneuvering around the blocks and barriers to your connection with your Source.

Art-making, especially in the form of a visual image, will help you in one instance, objectify the obstacles that are keeping you from plugging in fully to your Higher Self. Then, you can see where they are located and what they look like. The art is also helpful in putting form, color and movement to dream images and meditation experiences. So much of what comes from out of your subconscious is in the form of images and feelings. Words often don't do your Innerworld justice, but the image holds such profound, metaphorical meaning with practical applications and implications for your life.

What I recommend is that you keep an art journal too. This can be included within your journal where you write your thoughts. However, best yet, get a separate journal dedicated to this tool. I like the art drawing books available at craft stores that are bound and have thick paper, perfect for use with any sort of media. Keep on hand anything from markers, crayons, chalk pastels, colored pencils to paints. Explore. Find what media you enjoy using. Remember, this is yet another tool to support you on your path of finding what tools and techniques help you to plug into your Higher Self.

Here are some suggestions for you to use as a starting point when you are ready to dive into art-making. The most important message I can share with you about your art is that this tool is not about creating a beautiful end result. Instead, it should be approached from that part of you who remembers being in kindergarten, just playing with the colors and their marks on the paper for pure pleasure. A large part of being able to feel your connection with your guides, Higher Self and Source is found in your capacities for child-like innocence. Children don't have the filters and inhibitions the adults have, instead they welcome surprise, fun and play. So, approach your art-making with such abandon. After all, you aren't going to be graded or encouraged to hang your art expressions on the refrigerator—unless you want to!

Use art-making to explore the images and experiences you encounter in the Underworld. Draw what you feel is holding you back. Draw your obstacles. Draw what treasures you find along this alchemical path. Use color, shapes and movement across the page, expressing your experiences. Draw what it feels like to meditate. Draw what your relationship to your Higher Self looks and feels like. Draw the dream that perplexes you. Draw the guide you encountered within your waking dream. As always with creativity, the possibilities are endless and the experiences reveal your uncovered magnificence.

PART 5

THE UPPERWORLD

You are not a drop in the ocean. You are the entire ocean, in a drop.
—Rumi, You Are

THE RUBEDO

The Rubedo is the final phase of alchemy and occurs within the realm of the Upperworld. This phase works through the connection and commitment you made with your Higher Self—with Source. You have been working with transcending your erroneous beliefs and feelings from the personality, the ego, the Underworld, and now you are working with your spiritual transformation. Although you are working with Spirit, you never leave the cycles of life. Your feet remain on the ground, while you still venture in and out of the Underworld, as life is always happening. It's important to remember when you are at this stage that you understand you are a fallible human, having not escaped death, decay and rebirth. However, for having ventured forth, you know how better to traverse the various worlds and bring with you your golden thread, your inner light. You know that everything is woven together, interconnected by this thread of gold, created by your thoughts and your feelings.

The Rubedo stage is referred to as the reddening and is a continuation of the Albedo transformation. With the discovery of the inner light from within the Underworld—within your unconscious— you must use this light so it becomes ever present to your conscious Self. This is the stage where the Alchemist accepts his spiritual inheritance. He knows himself to be of a Divine Essence and this conscious awareness of his divinity is evolving toward permanency. He is plugged in more than not and he co-creates his world.

The Alchemist viewed the process of Rubedo, the reddening, the red stone, in three stages: Fermentation, Distillation and Coagulation

Fermentation

Fermentation is the fifth operation in a series of seven operations that comprises the work of the Alchemists. Fermentation is the first stage of Rubedo in which the Above inspires the heart of the Alchemist to maintain the newly found infusion of energies within. The process of Fermentation has two phases with the first involving the phase of putrefaction or decomposition. This decomposition is the rotting of the dead Self. On a deep level, there is realization of your deficiencies and the need to look into the dark shadows of yourself and face what you most deny. Carl Jung spoke of the importance of embracing one's shadow so the darkness of it could be illuminated. When the shadow is embraced, it can be healed by the introspection of what gave it birth. This is the second phase of Fermentation when the extinction of the old Self and obsolete ways of being is resurrected into its new form, with a new psychic Center. Regeneration and new growth begins.

You know that you have succeeded with Fermentation when the stage of yellowing occurs. You must go beyond the whitening and enter into the yellowing. This is your first hint that you are making **GOLD**! This golden warmth appears when you allow the spirit in (in-spiritos) from the Above to occur within your imagination Below, within your Secret Fire of the inspired imagination.

In alchemical terms, sulfur and mercury must come together to create the One Stone. Sulfur is the yang, the masculine energy, and considered the fiery, active Sun combined from the elements of Fire and Air. Mercury is yin, the feminine energy, and considered the watery, passive Moon combined from the elements of Water and Earth. Fusing the Sun and Moon (King and Queen) together is the

KEY to the entire work of alchemy and the meaning to the symbol of the ouroboros—the snake biting its own tail. The snake circles back to its tail, biting it to represent the flow of opposites that are now, eternally flowing into one another and indistinguishable at higher levels of the alchemical work.

The Will and the Imagination work together at this stage to know Source. This is done, as we have been discussing throughout this book, by using the tools and techniques discovered in the Innerworld. A Fermented person becomes suddenly alive and irrepressibly hopeful because now their attention is focused on aspirations that are grander and out of this world. You expose your own internal spirit to receive the divine spirit of All That Is. This is when there is a union of your body with soul and spirit. Often in this stage, the Alchemist communicates with the unseen realm, with such beings as the Higher Self, spirits, angels and guides.

Distillation

Distillation is the sixth operation in a series of seven operations that comprises the work of the Alchemists. Distillation is the second stage of Rubedo. In this operation you undergo a repeated separation and recombination of the parts of the personality that no longer work with the new Self that has been uncovered. As a human being, you grow attached to the material world along with your beliefs, thoughts and feelings. This stage of the work calls upon you to release attachment to everything and feel detachment as a true form of peace and well-being. You learn to feel detachment as a true form of love. This form of love is from a higher level of connection with All That Is. You can only practice this way of being when you can release your attachments to outcomes or to the future of events and circumstances. Distillation helps wash away the dark matter of attachment and reveal the deeper, intuitive Self in its purest form of trust. Now the Alchemist is trusting in the provisions from the Source.

Distillation simultaneously takes place on three levels of experience: the physical, the mental and the spiritual. This is seen in the vertical axis of reality, whereas our awareness travels to the Above and Below and back again just like Hermes Trismegestus taught and his magical wand, the caduceus, represented.

Coagulation

Coagulation is the seventh and final operation of the entire alchemical process that comprises the work of the Alchemists. Coagulation is the final stage of Rubedo. Sulfur and Mercury working at this higher level create the coagulated salt that forms the Philosopher's Stone, which is the permanent state of Golden Consciousness. This level of consciousness transcends both heaven and earth, joining spirit and soul with the body, separating them from everything that would hinder their ascension into the union with the Divine. This is the stage of the phoenix rising from the ashes, symbolizing the complete resurrection. The person that has successfully accomplished this stage has completed unification within oneself on all levels. Although most do not reach this stage, it provides a glimpse into the possibilities.

CHAPTER XII
Deepening Connections

Exercise Your Higher Self

Once I found myself extending the amount of time I was able to remain plugged into my Higher Self, I decided to exercise creative rights with the process. I thought to myself if I can refocus myself during most anytime of the day and return to that conscious intention of finding my reconnection, finding my Center again, then maybe I could extend it to include "off the beaten path" moments. You know, those moments you really don't think matter. To me, these moments include routine tasks, such as exercising. I could already receive a high or rush of endorphins when I exercised, but now, I would literally ask my Higher Self, the Spirit Friends and Source to join me. To them, this was an amusing request as they tell me that they are always with me. Well, okay, yes this is true, but most often I was oblivious to this fact. So, I asked that they humored me and away I went, consciously aligning with them and asking them to join me during these activities. Every walk, every Zumba class and every mile on the elliptical, I requested their presence.

Although they are always with me, as they are always with you, if we don't at least acknowledge this, we won't recognize this. So, you ask me why does this matter? I will share with you that the more we learn to extend our ability of existing from a place of being plugged into our Higher Self—Guides and Source—the more conscious clarity we will have within our lives. When we are conscious, we make informed and wise choices in each and every moment that we are plugged in. Not only do our bodies benefit from this exercise, but also our inspiration benefits from exercising our intention to being plugged into our Center more often. We are propelled into knowing and exerting more of our greatness within. As the axiom teaches us "practice makes perfect," I have come to know this directly as a result of this process.

I want to share with you two resulting, pleasurable stories as examples of being plugged into my Higher Self, Center and Source during exercise. These experiences gifted me with deeply rewarding connections to life. The first story took place in San Clemente, California when I was jogging along the beach early one morning. It was very common for me to go to the beach and jog in the early morning hours of 5:30 or 6:00. During these times, I often had the beach as my private oasis. As usual, this particular morning, I was alone. While jogging along the beach, I was mesmerized by the serenity of the morning, observing my environment and feeling inspired by its beauty. It was low tide, the waves were light and calm and the crush of the wet sand to each stride felt like running on velvet. I was in the groove, moment to moment, and was feeling pure joy. There was nowhere else I wanted to be, but right there amidst the sights, sounds and smells of the beach and ocean. I felt the urge to stop in my tracks, turn and face the ocean and absorb its beauty some more. No sooner than I stopped and turned towards the ocean, two dolphins jumped out of the water right in front of me at the twelve o'clock position. They jumped so high; they cleared the water, creating an arch in the sky while they crossed each other in mid air, ending with a perfect landing back into the glass-like ocean. The display of their acrobatic feat was captivating, spectacular and inspirational. Their joyful play enfolded me in that moment. I quickly looked around to see if anyone else was nearby and possibly had witnessed this delightful sight. Not a soul in sight. Right then I knew that this incredible moment belonged to me and the dolphins and only us. Within our shared moment of reverence for the same beauty, I felt our interspecies' communion.

The second story took place in California's Dana Point Harbor located a few miles from my home. Quite often, I drive to the harbor to take walks around the marina, viewing the boats and the marine life that live amongst the waterways. I intentionally invited my Guides and Higher Self to accompany me. Although they are technically ever-present, it brought awareness to their presence by means of my invitation. They gladly accepted and off we went on our walk. I decided to view this repetitive walk from new eyes. I hosted an inner conversation with them, as they proceeded to fill me with ideas for this book. Every time "we" would go out walking, the sights, the sounds and the hellos from passersby were always more colorful and cheerful. When I walk with this conscious connection and communion, it feels as if I am taller in stature and my perspective of the environment has expanded. It's as if I fill a larger dimensional space, while I am walking. I am more observant and sense more about nature when connected to Source than those times when I do not make that conscious connection.

During this particular walk, I was purposely expanding my awareness as far out of my body as I could make it go without loosing mindfulness of my Center. I came to a set of stairs, jogged up them and ascended to the bridge, which took me over the central waterway where the boats travel in, around and through the harbor. I reached the center of the bridge and felt an inclination to stop and look down about thirty feet to the water. No sooner than I stopped, I heard a blow of air, which sounded like a dolphin breeching and gathering the next breath of air. I was looking in the right direction and there I saw them, two dolphins breeching and submerging. Watching the spot where I saw them in the water next to a docked forty-foot boat, they reemerged. They were shallowly swimming through the harbor. As many times as I have walked around the harbor over the past fifteen years, I never once had witnessed dolphins swimming within this space. Yet, there they were. A man walked up to me inquiring if I had just seen the two dolphins. Apparently, he spotted them as well. We engaged in conversation about why they were there. He proceeded to tell me it's a rare sight to catch a glimpse of them when they enter the harbor. He said that the female dolphins would enter the harbor in pairs when one of them is ready to give birth. The accompanying female dolphin assists the expectant mother by keeping her safe from predators while she is birthing her new young. They work together to bring forth new life then return to the greater ocean. He told me that he had seen a few of these dolphin couples, mother and her midwife, within the harbor confines, but that indeed, it is a rare sight. I was feeling honored and connected, yet once again, to the beauty of life found in the moment when I am aligned with Source.

There are countless other stories to share, but I know you get my point, for you too have experienced moments of being at the right place at the right time and feeling the connection. We can encourage more of these moments to happen when we acknowledge them. Know that when these beautiful moments occur, you are allowing yourself to externally witness the interconnectedness of yourself within. When you are connected with your Center, the Source within, you are welcoming the greater interconnectivity with Source—All That Is—within your life.

Connect with your Guides

I will let you in on a secret. Your Higher Self, guides and angels are already plugged into Source, for these energies never left Source. They are of Source, which is God. Our tendency is to view our interaction with them as being separate from ourselves. This is a limited view of their dynamic interrelationship with us, with each other and with Source. When you open to allow these connections and communications, quite naturally you are simply choosing to experience the multidimensional qualities of Source within your world. Source is pervasive.

The guides, angels and guardians come to assist us in our memory and our interrelationship with All That Is. They want us to know that Source is ever-present within us already. They say that they are a collection of many minds, considered as one, emanating from Source. Not only are they one; all of us are one and all of us come from the Source. They speak of vibration and frequency, distinguishing the relationship: "We are vibration. Flowers are vibration. Frequency separates." They are just of a different vibration from us, which allows them to move more easily through time. Yet, everything in the universe is of vibration. We share that commonality. However, frequency is determined by how often the vibration repeats itself within a specified time. Therefore, we are connected to our spirit friends through vibrations, but are separate from them in our rate of vibration. When they communicate with us, we must raise our vibrations to a higher and more encompassing frequency in order to hear and feel them. The more we practice connecting and communicating with higher sources of vibration, we learn to elevate our frequency in that moment. In order to maintain the momentum of these higher frequencies, we need to practice what we are learning.

You will strengthen the connection with your guides by spending time in your thoughts. Practices of regular and consistent prayer, meditation, contemplation, reflection or journaling help strengthen you in your awareness of this connection. While writing this book, HEALING SPIRIT, also known as my Higher Self, told me to spend much time in thought as "they" (my Spirit Friends) would support me in the process of writing. They required my focus and clarity of direction in order to present themselves to my conscious awareness within my thoughts, while I was writing this book. This is one way they enter our conscious awareness, through the mechanism of thoughts. Their words and information comes into our awareness as packages of thought as they download information into our minds. They also enter our awareness through other sensory receptors, such as through our physiology.

You will become aware of your guides, angels and guardians when you release any and all expectations for how you think they should be interacting with you. Let go of the preconceived ideas for communication. Instead, be open to anything because truly anything happens within their realm of vibration. In the beginning, they may make their presence known to you through symbolic messages; these can include a book that was given to you, a person you meet or an email you receive that provides you with a personal message. Remember, they are and have always been around you. It's just that now you are open to them. They can help orchestrate events and present themselves as animals. They will take any form that is most comfortable for you.

You will allow your guides' direct communications within your mind as you continue to grow in your awareness of their presence and practice consistent meditation. Silencing your mind and being still creates the space for their gentle presence and soft voices to be heard. It takes time and practice. They are ready and available, but you must invite them to make this form of communication. My suggestion for commencing this form of communication before you meditate is to write in your journal your intentions to remain open to receiving their messages. Go into meditation. When you are finished, go back to your journal and write your experiences about your meditation. Then, ask your guides for their message. Allow the message to write through your own penmanship. Yes, this will feel contrived at first, but after time, the communications can develop into a form of automatic writing. Obviously for me, the Ouija Board has been one of my "automatic" ways for being in communication with my guides. However, I also practice journaling to hear them and I practice meditation, which allows them to present their messages within my thoughts. Just know that they will continue to present themselves to you within many ways as long as you remain open to the possibilities.

Know Infinite Possibilities

As you plug into your Higher Self with growing consistency, you'll be shown with greater clarity that everything is alive and interconnected. When this realization becomes the path of your life, everything becomes communication and everything has meaning.

You will find your Innerworld is directly connected with the Outerworld and the Outerworld will speak directly to your Innerworld. You will begin to notice that your entire reality is alive and conscious, while everything is in constant communication and collaboration—the origin of synchronicity.

Divinity

Always know that you are a Divine Being that is committedly connected to your Higher Self. Through the process of introspection, reflection and contemplation you are clearing away the debris of the old Self that stands in the way of honoring this connection. Continue the work you have been doing in order to support your conscious alignment with your Higher Self.

Alignment is always a breath away. Take a deep breath, relax and ease into your Center. Your meditation sessions support this alignment in the grandest of ways, as you continue to clear the clutter from your mind during these sessions. The more you can find stillness in your thoughts, the better able you are to receive new thoughts. Try to be still and just listen. Allow without any preconceived ideas.

When you feel those times of struggle, while trying to come back to your Center—your Higher Self—open yourself to grace. Ask for divine assistance from Source, from God, to help you in this process. All aspects of Source relish your request for help. Your helpers are ever-present, waiting in the wings to assist you in remembering your divinity. They want you to be connected to your Center, thus plugged into your Higher Self. However, they can't interfere and do the work for you. You must do the work as we have been discussing in this book and they, who are truly an aspect of you and Source, are able to reach you more effectively.

Awareness

Allow yourself to remain open, receptive and aware of your environment. This means actively engaging the Divine Feminine within and embracing these principles within your day-to-day life. Observe, notice and remember to breathe. Use your breath to slow you down so you can notice yourself within you environment. Try to take breaks several times throughout your day and just take three deep breaths. Then, wait. Notice. Feel.

When you practice staying aware, your life comes alive in colorful, synchronistic ways. Even though synchronicity is always around you, since it is the connective golden thread of the universe, you can learn to notice it more often. When we don't notice these events, we tend to label these synchronistic moments as "miracles" and believe they are outside of our reach. Then, we take a step back from Source. That's because we don't understand our interconnectivity with All That Is. When you are determined to give yourself to your connection with Source and you are willing to receive the gifts, synchronistic phenomena become the staple of your life. The right people, things and circumstances are showing up, just perfectly timed, but now you are noticing. Being aware and noticing is the sign to Source that you appreciate your connection to All That Is. As you allow this awareness to grow, you will continue noticing countless ways you and others are being gifted. It represents the premise that there is a Divine Order so interdependent and interconnected with All That Is that it translates to understanding the importance of each and every life in relationship to the other and to the next.

We are constantly receiving messages from everywhere and working to remain open to the multitude of places these messages do present themselves. You may receive your message from a seemingly random person you bump into while shopping and notice that what is in this person's shopping cart is the precise item for which you are searching. They are able to direct you to it. You may overhear a conversation between two friends standing in line at the post office and their conversation includes details that bring clarity to an issue with which you have been struggling. While driving your car, you may hear a song on the radio, see a billboard or view a license plate that shares a very personal and pertinent message to you, answering a question you had.

Read your environment by observing the themes that emerge, as small as they seem. You may notice a series of red tailed hawk sightings along your drive to work that week, although you haven't seen even one in that area for over a year. Ask yourself what this type of hawk represents to you. Engage assistance to understand its meaning by researching it further online. Remember, your Outerworld is not disconnected from your Innerworld. The themes you experience in the external landscape roll over into your dreamscape and vice-a-versa. Since you are already recording your dreams, you are able to make the connection between that dream you just had where a hawk appeared to you, to the series of sightings of the hawks on your way to work. Since everything is interconnected, life is full of surprises with meaning and purpose.

Notice the connections, all the while allowing them to unfold into new levels of understanding as one's gnosis grows and develops through more life experiences. Allow meaning to infinitely unfold. Since we are truly multidimensional beings, existing in physical form, spiritual form and divine form, all at the same time, know that these types of events will always carry multiple meanings. So look at them from the hawk's view; it's always a larger picture. When you can glimpse the bigger picture of synchronistic events happening to you and around you, you are more readily prepared to accept that even those tough events that are happening are also coming from a place of cosmic orchestration, assisting the evolution of your soul.

Opportunity

Every experience in life is an opportunity. Your Higher Self relishes this notion, as experience is the natural flow of the universe. Since experience continually presents itself in countless ways from varying directions, you are constantly offered infinite opportunities. We must remember to recognize these opportunities in their guises. They may appear as the procession of events that lead to the timely sale of your home when the market was seller favorable, thus garnering you top dollar for it. In turn, that may have left you open to traveling across the country, to finding your new dream job and now you are unencumbered to make that move. Also, they can appear in the guise of the spouse who initiated divorce, leaving you behind in a trail of tears of heartbreak and betrayal. Yet, later down the road you realize it was a blessing in disguise, allowing you to leave deception behind and move toward authenticity with yourself and others.

Your job is to become aware of these presenting conditions and see them for their truths. While they can appear extremely tough and trying, at first glance, and maybe even just as tough after many glances, they always show up as agents of change for your soul evolution. The hard times push you to change and move outside of your comfort zones, but the impact is much grander. Every so-called crisis contains the seeds of an opportunity found in its polar opposite to how you might at first perceive it. As you remain open, a bigger picture reveals the presence of its opportunity found within the hardship, because the universe reminds you that flow is perfectly balanced in the paradox of opposites.

Every crisis and every opportunity, whether it's related to your health, finances, or personal experience is truly a litmus test, offering you a peek into your progress with your inner work. It shines a light upon the areas within you that require your attention to review. Questions emerge asking you what inner qualities are being evoked and what fears do you need to embrace. The meaning of these questions is found in its invitation for you to bring more of yourself into the light, including more expressions of compassion, dedication, understanding, truth, trust, authenticity and the list goes on. Know that opportunity is ubiquitous when the blinders are removed.

Raise Your Frequency

Gratitude

Expressing your gratitude is one of the most powerful frequencies of love, as it comes directly from your heartfelt Center. When you freely share your appreciation for another, for nature, for the cosmos, you develop a greater sense of connection to your surroundings. Not only does it feel good to be on the receiving end of appreciation, the one who extends it also receives. The frontal regions of the brain are activated producing dopamine and serotonin—the feel good chemicals—that suffuse the body. The more you practice gratitude, your well-being and happiness increase. You raise your vibration and open yourself to more abundance.

Start and end your day with a gratitude statement. For what are you grateful? You can state it as a prayer to God or as a statement to the universe. Appreciate your current life and all that it entails. Give thanks for the people who are in your life, including the ones who "push" your buttons. Remember, they bring you to discover your greater Self. Give thanks for the lessons you are learning. Give thanks to your seen and unseen friends, guides and angels. Give thanks to those you have not yet met for they will come as messengers and helpers, supporting your efforts. Give thanks when you are amidst hardship because you know that it always appears to assist you in your evolution.

During each day, go out of your way to say thank you to others. Thank the clerk at the store when you buy your groceries. Thank your children's teachers at school. Thank the person driving that car in traffic who lets you into their lane. Although that driver can't hear your verbal thanks, they will see your wave of thanks. Call someone out of the blue just to thank that person. The object of your gratitude does not even need to be present for the effects to work, for gratitude works much like the power of prayer. With every positive thought of appreciation that is sent, a loving, vibratory spiral expands out into the universe, attracting like and increasing in size. It's a win-win for all involved.

Vibration

You are supported in the paradox of the universe. The thoughts and feelings you transmit about yourself are always received without judgment by the universe and are lovingly and unconditionally supported. Although you may want abundance in wealth, for example, deep down within yourself you believe and feel that you are unworthy of such bounty. Instead, you will experience precisely what you think and feel deep down about yourself and your situation. You are unconditionally supported to experience and receive the reality that matches your energetic vibration of what you believe to be true. That is the paradox.

Everything within the world is energy and has its own vibration, including a belief or belief system. The experiences you attract to yourself match your existing belief system. Just look at your experiences and you will know what you believe. If you don't like your experiences, then change your beliefs, at the level of your thoughts and feelings, by returning to your inner work. Observe what holds your current beliefs captive. Seek what would help expand your limited or inhibited beliefs. Ask the question of yourself and listen for the answer. Your Higher Self knows. Ask for guidance and be prepared to receive it in a dream, a meditation or possibly through a message sent directly from the universe found in a song. Remember, there are infinite possibilities to the ways you are supported by Source.

When you support your desired reality with your conscious awareness and intentions, the relationship with yourself develops at a creative level. No longer do you blame anything outside of yourself for your experiences. It is out of this blossoming understanding that the quality of the relationship you create with yourself, gives birth to your entire world of form and experience. In other words, your world is a reflection of you and organizes itself around the energy field you have consciously created and continue to create.

You are intimately related to the world of your experiences. You are the co-creator in this pervasive and dynamic interrelatedness of everything. You are continually creating and recreating your world as your internal perspectives shift and change. Life blossoms from your feelings at every given moment. Observe the moment. Notice what you feel. Shift your perspective to find joy in that moment. Now repeat that within a spiral of many moments strung together. You are the co-creator of your life and of your world. Choice is how you strive to create a life of joy.

CHAPTER XIII
Hologram of the Whole

Nature of Source

There is the One. It is from within the One that everything descends and into the One everything ascends. The Alchemists call it the One Thing. The quest for the Philosopher's Stone teaches the knowledge of the One Thing. The descent into the darkest depths of Self births the ascent of the Divine Self. They are truly One and the same, connected by the Golden Light—the Light of Source, which is the Light of your Secret Fire.

The Alchemists understood and still understand where this One Thing resides. It has and it will always reside as the signature of God within you. When you believe that this power is outside of yourself, whether you call this power demons, angels or Higher Self, you separate yourself from this single guiding light. Yes, there is a greater Source appearing outside of you; just look around and see the world. Yet at the same time, that Source is precisely what comprises you. You are an aspect of that greater Source. Think of yourself as a hologram of this Source. You are a living expression of this light in physical form. You are the particle and the wave. Remember, everything that occurs in the Below has its correspondence in the Above.

Fractal geometry shows us that within a fragment of nature, an overall recursive pattern of similarity and often one of exactitude, exists within the larger form of itself. So what may appear to be disconnected and irregular fragments without a relationship to the whole, in essence is a relationship with a higher order of continuity. What appears to be chaos is truly an organized pattern found within scales of the chaotic form. Likewise, the development of our consciousness is inherently fractal. Our task as the Alchemist is to recognize this higher, hidden order found within the parts of our consciousness and produce a continuity of consciousness within our very being.

The collective unconscious is shifting to a collective consciousness. What was once unconscious and impervious to our awareness is coming back into our awareness on a larger scale, awakening this awareness worldwide within the minds and hearts of many. This is the inherent pattern that is emerging. We are noticing what is working and what is not working so well. Many are taking action by making not only big changes in the world, but are also making changes right at home. Change for the better truly does begin with one. It begins with you. As you awaken to your heart, your Center, your Higher Self, others around you cannot help but be affected by it. As you clean out your closet and make amends with the discarded, you shift awareness by another degree within the Great Spiral of life.

Biologist Rupert Sheldrake coined the term "Morphogenic Field" to explain his theory of an underlying energy field of consciousness that serves as a collective memory for a given species. This field is created by all living species and acts as an organizing principle, influencing the behavior and activity of the related species. Thought and emotional patterns constantly contribute to the development of this energy field, affecting how the species will continue to develop. We also draw these morphic fields to us through the quality of our own resonance. As we strive to transform the dross of our lives, we are automatically assisted in this endeavor because like resonance within this collective field attracts to the transformed energy we have created. On a larger scale, this theory suggests that if enough people are thinking, feeling and acting in a similar way or with a common goal, this could possibly create a ripple effect, creating a field of similarity that influences the rest of humanity.

Have you noticed the recent growth and serge in popularity of the paranormal ghost hunting shows on television? There are also a multitude of streaming podcast shows on the Internet dedicated to the paranormal, the unseen and the unexplained. There are other shows that explore angels, cryptozoology, aliens and mediumship. Other popular shows on television include personality psychics who reach out to the dead and bring comfort to the living. What was once old becomes new again and the consciousness of humanity has spiraled out once again to shed light on these topics that fascinated the curious minds of our ancestors too.

We are now searching deeper than ever before and are sharing our finds worldwide through the webs of the Internet and social media. We are awaking the Divine Feminine within humanity as we continue to search deeply within her domain of the unknown. We seek to find what is really looming within her darkness and what is beyond. She is the mistress of the imaginal and welcomes us once again to share in her great mysteries not only within the world as we search for ghosts, but in our Innerworlds as we learn to make peace with our demons and uncover our daemons. She knows that the two go hand in hand. As we continue down this path of exploration, we bring her back to the forefront of our consciousness. She returns to the land of the living and unites within our awareness, gifting us with clarity to the seen and the unseen forces.

The Great Cycle

Everything is cyclical, exhibiting patterns of death, decay then rebirth. For the sake of integrity, this natural process repeats itself, gaining its momentum and strength from this endless cycle, spiraling up into a greater awareness of itself at each turn. This is evolution at its finest, continually born out of this inevitability of change. Welcome change as it positions you for evolutionary growth every time it enters your life, as change provides the required nutrients that feed your soul.

The stories I shared within this book are not just my stories. They are your stories too as they are universal. All of us have magical, synchronistic and inspirational stories that constantly unfold, while encircling us in wisdom, throughout our lives. Now, it is your turn to reach into your story. Take time to explore the memories this book shook loose within your psyche. Connect the dots and deepen into your journey. Support the hologram of your life by further welcoming the mystical. Develop the intuitive and psychic abilities that already reside within you and within the morphic field of human abilities. Tap into this realm and share it out loud.

Always remember that you are a magnificent, Divine Spiritual Being, capable of momentous feats, as you came here to demonstrate your abilities and capabilities for creating your world at every moment. You are a god, an aspect of the capital GOD. You are a hologram of the whole. You are a microcosm of the macrocosm and you continually shift roles as you move through the great cycle of life—death, decay and rebirth. As Above, so Below; so Below, as Above.

This axiom of correspondence was further brought to my awareness one evening, as my Board Operator partner and I were finishing up a session with the Spirit Friends. The conversation was about the path of clarity. In the process of thanking them for their inspired communication, I told them that they are "my great Alchemist Masters, our true mentors in every way" and they said, "and you are our mentors too." That which is above is the same as that which is below. We are in this together.

Reunion

Many years have passed since that first spontaneous meeting between DAKi and dear Little One. So much of life has been lived and so much has transpired. Dear Little One could never have understood the impact, half a century earlier, that their fateful encounter would have inspired and foreshadowed her life's path. All came to fruition because of one little angelic sprite making certain his little human friend would remember whence she came.

Remarkable memories awaken within the all-knowing light of Source. "DAKi, is that you? DAKi, is that really you?" I said with disbelief as I opened my eyes within the light. "It is I," DAKi replied. "You really came back to me after all of these years?" I said in pure astonishment. DAKi, in his naturally calm demeanor said:

Dear Little One, I never left you. We never go away; we just fade into the background until the time comes for the reunion.

I even left you with a signature of myself that was carried within your moniker all these years, enacting as a key, little by little unlocking further memory of your Divine Light.

My mind was spinning, trying to reveal just what that key could be. What could DAKi have left with me that had escaped my detection other than the extraordinary, yet faded memory of our friendship? DAKi whispered in my ear, "Look to the initials of your name and there "i" have always been—existing with my KAD! My name is an anadrome of your initials." My jaw dropped open in disbelief. I had never noticed that before and now I was reveling in absolute wonder, amazement and an even greater sense of confidence that speaks to our incredible friendship and connection. "Yes, I am the wee little "i" right outside of KAD and that is where I have always been and will always be," exclaimed DAKi.

Now, it's time, for the moment is upon us. Sit back and listen closely as I retell your favorite story about the Golden Light. Know that this story I told to you when you were young speaks directly to **your journey** and quite frankly, it's reminiscent of everyone's journey! Now, feel yourself within it.

DAKi knew precisely where the story was leading and this time the story would change. So, DAKi, trying not to give away this new plan, straightened his posture, sat up tall and steadfast, while he took a deep breath, closed his eyes and chanted in his wee little voice:

Golden beholden the bright shimmering light
While all angels enamor in this delight
Of coveted dreams from one little sprite
To discover gold hidden within plain sight.

To journey so far yet remain so near
Seeking heaven above within this sphere
Venture down deeply with tricksters austere
Oh dear Little One could I be more clear?

Just close your eyes, but don't fall asleep
To the shut-eye world of counting sheep
Or becoming one of the herd, Bo-peep
Hold steadfast instead to this light you seek.

With its golden blaze as bright as the sun
And its lunar reflection being second to none
When the transit of Venus has just begun
Know not to fear where the planets have spun.

Go into the bowels of the earth instead
Eyes open wide to the dross from the lead
Life is found in what we may think to be dead
Just dig deeper to uncover that golden thread.

Golden beholden shine that bright inner light
On the depths where demons make havoc and fright
Their messages all twisted around will incite
Internal paradoxical treasures to unite.

So transcend each moment and there you will find
The cross road, the center axis, the tree of life all align
When the Above and the Below are together entwined
The heart of your being creates a golden state of mind.

Golden beholden, my dear Little One
This story is about **YOU**, I've told in fun
Welcome back to gnosis where it all begun
Our friendship is lasting and never undone.

Know **YOU ARE Golden**, a spirit shining bright
As your soul is a hologram of Source Light
Revealing yourself through every plight
For **YOU ARE the Gold** found within plain sight.

And this, my dear friend, is your Golden Light, which is your Golden Key to the Universe—to Source. Now, fly, as you are a god amongst gods and your world has been awaiting your return.

Glossary

Albedo – known as the white stone, it is the second phase of three phases of the alchemical transformation when a light appears within the darkness and impurities are washed away.

All That Is – the divine essence that comprises the eternal universal matrix of everything. It is all of creation.

Center – the alignment to Source within.

Daemon – a type of guardian spirit from Source.

Hieros Gamos – the sacred marriage of the internal and eternal King and Queen principles, infused by the divine essence of God.

Innerworld – the internal world within our personal psyche in which we are conscious.

Lesser Stone – the offspring born from the merging of the masculine and feminine energies within nature, which will eventually be united with the powers of the Above to create the Greater Stone, known as the Philosopher's Stone.

Nigredo – known as the "darkening," it is the first phase of three phases of the alchemical transformation when one immerses into the darkness and chaos of the Underworld.

Outerworld – the day-to-day world that we personally inhabit.

Philosopher's Stone – in general, this Stone is the universal spirit that is present within everything, including everyone. It is present at the beginning of the Great Work and at the very end of it; it is the symbol of man perfected; it is the end result of the alchemical work.

Rubedo – known as the red stone, also contains the "citrinitas phase" where the light of consciousness occurs, is is the last of the three phases of the alchemical transformation. Creating gold and the Philosopher's Stone signals the success of this stage.

Source – the omnipotent and omnipresent universal source from which all of creation came. God.

The Great Work – an ongoing spiritual practice of self-purification through the transmutation of unwanted emotions and thoughts, resulting in the mystical union of Self with Source.

Underworld – the internal world within our personal psyche in which we are unconscious.

Upperworld – the metaphorical and spiritual world we inhabit where we are consciously aware of our connection with Source.

Bibliography

Al-Rawi, Rosina-Fawzia B. *Grandmother's Secrets: The Ancient Rituals and Healing Power of Belly Dancing*. Trans. Monique Arav. New York: Interlink, 1999. Print.

Avens, Roberts. *Imagination Is Reality: Western Nirvana in Jung, Hillman, Barfield, and Cassirer*. Irving, TX: Spring Publications, 1980. Print.

Bonheim, Jalaja. *The Serpent and the Wave: A Guide to Movement Meditation*. Berkeley, CA: Celestial Arts, 1992. Print.

Childre, Doc Lew, Howard Martin, and Donna Beech. *The HeartMath Solution*. San Francisco, CA: HarperSanFrancisco, 1999. Print.

Dahlman, Karen A. *The Spirits of Ouija: Four Decades of Communication*. San Clemente, CA: Creative Visions Publications, 2013. Print.

Dance, Richard. "Hermeticism, Gnosticism, and Neoplatonism Non-Attachment: A Key to Salvation in the Ancient Western Esoteric Tradition." *Richard Dance Academic Papers: 1997 Comparative Perennial Philosophy of the Classical East & West*. Richard Dance, 17 Mar. 2012. Web. Fall 2014. <http://rdacademic.blogspot.com/2012/03/on-hermeticism-gnosticism-and.html>.

Edinger, Edward F. *Anatomy of the Psyche: Alchemical Symbolism in Psychotherapy*. La Salle, IL: Open Court, 1985. Print.

Flower, Michael A. *The Seer in Ancient Greece*. Berkeley: U of California, 2008. Print.

Gillabel, Dirk. "House of the Sun: Esoteric and Spiritual Articles." *House of the Sun: Esoteric and Spiritual Articles*. Dirk Gillabel. Web.

Fall 2014. <http://www.soul-guidance.com/houseofthesun/index.htm>.

Hauck, Dennis William. *The Emerald Tablet: Alchemy for Personal Transformation*. New York: Penguin/Arkana, 1999. Print.

Jacobson, Lyle. "The Binary Universe." *The Binary Universe and the Power of Nothing*. Lyle Jacobson, 2006. Web. Summer 2014. <http://www.anthonyrtaylor.com/binaryuniversetheorem/index.html>.

Johnson, Robert A. *Owning Your Own Shadow: Understanding the Dark Side of the Psyche*. San Francisco: HarperSanFrancisco, 1991. Print.

Lanza, Robert P., and Bob Berman. *Biocentrism: How Life and Consciousness Are the Keys to Understanding the True Nature of the Universe*. Dallas, TX: BenBella, 2009. Print.

Mandelbrot, Benoit B. *The Fractal Geometry of Nature*. New York: Freeman, 1983. Print.

McLean, Adam. "The Alchemy Web Site." *The Alchemy Web Site*. Dan Levy, 1996. Web. Fall 2014. <http://www.alchemywebsite.com/index.html>.

Melchizedek, Drunvalo. *The Ancient Secret of the Flower of Life*. Vol. 1. Flagstaff, AZ: Light Technology Pub, 1990. Print.

"Nag Hammadi Library." *Nag Hammadi Library*. Ed. Lance S. Owens. Trans. Stephen Patterson and Marvin Meyer. Lance S. Owens, MD, 1995. Web. Jan.-Feb. 2015. <http://www.gnosis.org/naghamm/nhlintro.html>.

Pearlman, Ellen. *Tibetan Sacred Dance: A Journey into the Religious and Folk Traditions*. Rochester, VT: Inner Traditions, 2002. Print.

Perera, Sylvia Brinton. *Descent to the Goddess: A Way of Initiation for Women*. Toronto: Inner City, 1981. Print.

Pierrakos, Eva. *Creating Union: The Pathwork of Relationship*. Ed. Judith Saly. Madison, VA: Pathwork, 1993. Print.

Pierrakos, Eva. *The Pathwork of Self-transformation*. Ed. Judith Saly. New York: Bantam, 1990. Print.

Redmond, Layne. *When the Drummers Were Women: A Spiritual History of Rhythm*. New York: Three Rivers, 1997. Print.

Sheldrake, Rupert. "Morphic Fields and Morphic Resonance." *Noetic Now* 4 (2010). *Noetic Now Journal*. Institute of Noetic Sciences, Nov. 2010. Web. Feb. 2015. <http://www.noetic.org/noetic/>.

Starbird, Margaret. *The Goddess in the Gospels: Reclaiming the Sacred Feminine*. Rochester, VT: Bear & Company, 1998. Print.

Steinberg, Richard. "The Origin of the Word Daemon." *The Origin of the Word Daemon*. Take Our Word For It. Web. Feb. 2015. <http://ei.cs.vt.edu/~history/Daemon.html>.

Stoneman, Richard. *The Ancient Oracles: Making the Gods Speak*. New Haven, CT: Yale UP, 2011. Print.

Stross, Brian. "THE MESOAMERICAN SACRUM BONE: DOORWAY TO THE OTHERWORLD." MS. The University of Texas at Austin, Austin, Texas. *FAMSI*. Foundation for the Advancement of Mesoamerican Studies, INC. Web. Spring 2014. <http://www.famsi.org/index.html>.

Sugar, Oscar. "How the Sacrum Got Its Name." *JAMA: The Journal of the American Medical Association* 257.15 (1987): 2061-063. Print.

Taylor, Marjorie. *Imaginary Companions and the Children Who Create Them*. New York: Oxford UP, 1999. Print.

Ward, Dan S. "The Library of Halexandriah." *The Library of Halexandriah*. 21 Apr. 2003. Web. Summer 2014. <http://www.halexandria.org/home.htm>.

White, Stewart Edward. *The Betty Book.* 1st ed. New York: E.P. Dutton, 1937. *A Project Gutenberg of Australia EBook.* Project Gutenbert, Aug. 2003. Web. Summer 2014. <http://www.gutenberg.org>.

Winters, Carol. "The Feminine Principle: An Evolving Idea." *Quest Magazine* 94.5.NOV-DEC (2006): 206-15. *Theosophical Society in America.* The Kern Foundation. Web. <https://www.theosophical.org>.

Woodman, Marion, and Elinor Dickson. *Dancing in the Flames: The Dark Goddess in the Transformation of Consciousness.* Boston: Shambhala, 1996. Print.

About the Author

Karen A. Dahlman holds a master's degree from the University of New Mexico and is specialized in art psychotherapy, hypnosis and regression work. After spending her formative years living all over the United States, she made Southern California her home in 1999. Although she maintains her counseling licenses, she hung up her therapy shingle and entered the high tech. industry of telecommunications and founded CVC, Inc, a consulting and utility design firm for the fortune 500 wireless carriers, now in its fifteenth year of operation.

Within paranormal and metaphysical circles, Karen is known as a leading, expert Ouijaologist© who has been working directly with the Ouija Board since 1973 with consistently profound, spirit communications. She continues to deepen her interactions with the varying consciousness and sentient beings with whom she maintains relationships via this tool.

Having a strong, spiritual connection to her Spirit Friends, as she has throughout her entire life, Karen shares within her books the positive benefits of using the Ouija Board and other creative means as pathways for being in contact with the various spiritual dimensions that exist among us. Her writings teach us to discover our greatness within and find expression of this within the world for purposeful and meaningful life experiences.

Previous Work

The Spirits of Ouija: Four Decades of Communication
© Published 2013

The Spirit of Creativity: Embodying Your Soul's Passion
© Published 2012

Author Contact

PO Box 1496
San Clemente, CA 92674
karen@creativevisionspublications.com

Websites

creativevisionspublications.com
karenadahlman.com

Facebook

Karen A Dahlman

Twitter

@karenadahlman

Made in the USA
Lexington, KY
10 April 2016